coaching

Pearson

At Pearson, we have a simple mission: to help people make more of their lives through learning.

We combine innovative learning technology with trusted content and educational expertise to provide engaging and effective learning experiences that serve people wherever and whenever they are learning.

From classroom to boardroom, our curriculum materials, digital learning tools and testing programmes help to educate millions of people worldwide – more than any other private enterprise.

Every day our work helps learning flourish, and wherever learning flourishes, so do people.

To learn more, please visit us at **www.pearson.com**

brilliant

coaching
fourth edition

Become a manager who can coach

Julie Starr

 **Pearson**

Harlow, England • London • New York • Boston • San Francisco • Toronto • Sydney • Dubai • Singapore • Hong Kong
Tokyo • Seoul • Taipei • New Delhi • Cape Town • São Paulo • Mexico City • Madrid • Amsterdam • Munich • Paris • Milan

PEARSON EDUCATION LIMITED

KAO Two
KAO Park
Harlow CM17 9NA
United Kingdom
Tel: +44 (0)1279 623623
Web: www.pearson.com

First published 2008 (print)
Second edition published 2012 (print and electronic)
Third edition published 2017 (print and electronic)
Fourth edition published 2023 (print and electronic)

© Pearson Education Limited 2008 (print and electronic)
© Pearson Education Limited 2012, 2017, 2023 (print and electronic)

ISBN: 978-1-292-72556-7 (print)
        978-1-292-45727-7 (ePub)

British Library Cataloguing-in-Publication Data
A catalogue record for the print edition is available from the British Library

Library of Congress Cataloging-in-Publication Data
A catalog record for the print edition is available from the Library of Congress

10 9 8 7 6 5 4 3 2 1
27 26 25 24 23

Cover design by Two Associates
Print edition typeset in Plantin MT Pro 10/14pt by Straive
Printed by Ashford Colour Press Ltd, Gosport

NOTE THAT ANY PAGE CROSS REFERENCES REFER TO THE PRINT EDITION

Contents

Pearson's Commitment to Diversity, Equity and Inclusion

Pearson is dedicated to creating bias-free content that reflects the diversity, depth and breadth of all learners' lived experiences. We embrace the many dimensions of diversity including, but not limited to, race, ethnicity, gender, sex, sexual orientation, socioeconomic status, ability, age and religious or political beliefs.

Education is a powerful force for equity and change in our world. It has the potential to deliver opportunities that improve lives and enable economic mobility. As we work with authors to create content for every product and service, we acknowledge our responsibility to demonstrate inclusivity and incorporate diverse scholarship so that everyone can achieve their potential through learning. As the world's leading learning company, we have a duty to help drive change and live up to our purpose to help more people create a better life for themselves and to create a better world.

Our ambition is to purposefully contribute to a world where:

- Everyone has an equitable and lifelong opportunity to succeed through learning.
- Our educational products and services are inclusive and represent the rich diversity of learners.
- Our educational content accurately reflects the histories and lived experiences of the learners we serve.
- Our educational content prompts deeper discussions with students and motivates them to expand their own learning and worldview.

We are also committed to providing products that are fully accessible to all learners. As per Pearson's guidelines for accessible educational Web media, we test and retest the capabilities of our products against the highest standards for every release, following the WCAG guidelines in developing new products for copyright year 2022 and beyond. You can learn more about Pearson's commitment to accessibility at:

https://www.pearson.com/us/accessibility.html

While we work hard to present unbiased, fully accessible content, we want to hear from you about any concerns or needs regarding this Pearson product so that we can investigate and address them.

- Please contact us with concerns about any potential bias at:
  https://www.pearson.com/report-bias.html
- For accessibility-related issues, such as using assistive technology with Pearson products, alternative text requests, or accessibility documentation, email the Pearson Disability Support team at:
  disability.support@pearson

Acknowledgements

Along my learning journey, many people have contributed to the ideas and perspectives in this book and the related programmes we run for managers and leaders in the workplace. So, I would like to express gratitude for the work of the following people: Richard Bandler, Brandon Bays, Kevin Billett, Deepak Chopra, Dr Stephen Covey, Frank Daniels, Landmark Education, Milton H. Erickson, John Grinder, Byron Katie, Caroline Myss, M. Scott Peck, Anthony Robbins, Eckhart Tolle, Brian Tracey and Sir John Whitmore.

I'd also like to thank Eloise Cook and Rebecca Youé for their challenges, thoughts and ideas in preparation of the text.

Publisher's acknowledgements

23 Gallup, Inc: Employee Engagement on the Rise in the U.S. Jim Harter Gallup, Inc; 24 Aon plc: Aon Hewitt, Global Employee Engagement Levels Bounce Back To All-Time Highs In 2017, Aon plc; 24 United States Senate Committee on Health, Education, Labor and Pensions: Tamara Erickson, THE 21ST CENTURY WORKPLACE: PREPARING FOR TOMORROW'S EMPLOYMENT TRENDS TODAY 2005; 25 Mel Stark: Quoted by Mel Stark; 27 Gallup, Inc: What Is Employee Engagement and How Do You Improve It? Gallup.com; 32 Mary Parker Follett: Quoted by Mary Parker Follett; 52 Byron Katie: Quoted by Byron Katie; 52 Brandon Bays: Quoted by Brandon Bays; 64 Eckhart Tolle: Quoted by Eckhart Tolle; 92 Dr Wayne Dyer: Quoted by Dr Wayne Dyer.

About the author

Julie Starr is a coach, mentor, and facilitator with over 30 years of experience in raising the quality of everyday conversations in the workplace. Her simple methods and models shape manager and leader mindsets and behaviour globally. The founder of Starr Coaching, she is a passionate advocate of the need to shift the core principles that underpin collaboration at work.

Julie is also the author of *The Coaching Manual* (Pearson Education, 2021), which defines the principles and practice of personal coaching. Her book *The Mentoring Manual* (Pearson Education, 2021) helps to build effective mentor relationships. She also writes novels for Young Adults, *Magic to Memphis* (Ruffdogbooks, 2014) and Truth Keeper, (Ruffdogbooks, 2023). As well as regular speaking engagements, Julie provides coaching to senior leaders in the UK, Europe and beyond. To find out more, check out www.starrcoaching.co.uk and www.learnstarr.com

Introduction

Welcome to the fourth edition of *Brilliant Coaching*. This book focuses on one distinct application of coaching, namely, coaching by managers and leaders in the workplace. In particular, it focuses on how to adopt coaching principles and ideas to help others perform well in their role at work while building their skills or learning.

In this new edition, you'll find many of the previous methods and tools proven over almost 30 years of my, and my team's, work with this topic. You'll also find fresh information and routines, based on our continued study and practice in the field. For example, as working habits evolve, more managers must lead and manage virtual teams, as people more routinely work from home. The adoption of video conferencing is now commonplace, as a way of communicating and staying connected to colleagues. As a directly related point, how to maintain people's engagement and performance continues to be a challenge for all, as the impact of one upon the other is now clear. I'll cover engagement early on in Chapter 2 to illustrate how coaching is a critical link in the need to engage and enliven people at work.

We've also introduced free-to-download coaching materials in the online resources of our website www.LearnStarrcom. You'll find these located in the Free Resources area; for readers of *The Coaching Manual* and *The Mentoring Manual*, there are also specific free downloads for each book.

Get the most from your reading time

Why did you decide to pick up this book? Perhaps to gain further awareness and ability, or maybe to help you decide when and how to coach? Whatever your reasons, I'll say welcome. To help you get the most from your investment of time, let's take a look at how the book is designed to work.

About this book

The book is split into four parts:

● Part 1: Awareness

● Part 2: Ability

● Part 3: Application

● Part 4: Action

Here's how each of these parts will help you to adopt coaching principles and behaviours for yourself.

Part 1: Awareness – what is coaching and how does it work?

The first part of this book explains coaching in the context of an organisation or your workplace. You'll find clear definitions of what coaching is, and what it is not. We'll also examine what it means to be a manager or leader who coaches others, and how your mindset or attitude needs to shift. By reflecting on your own role, situation and challenges, we'll help you frame your own thinking and decide how coaching can work for you.

I will often talk to you as though you are already a manager and/or a leader. Please know that you do not have to have the formal role of manager to benefit from the ideas in this book. If you work in an environment where you have regular conversations with others, then the skills of coaching can benefit you. If you have a role where helping others to work smarter or to be more engaged and effective would really help, I'm confident that coaching has something to offer.

Part 2: Ability - what are the skills you need to develop?

In the second part of the book, we'll examine the main skills you'll need to develop, such as how to ask better questions and how to offer constructive feedback. Many of these skills are relevant outside of managing or coaching situations, as conversational skills, or general skills of life. I'll often use samples of dialogue or real-life examples to show how these skills look/sound in practice. To build on the ability you already have, I'll offer exercises or routines for you to try. Most of these exercises can be done 'undercover', so nobody needs to know what you're doing (many of us begin as covert coaches!).

Part 3: Application - how can you use coaching in your workplace?

In the third part, we'll look at principles and structures to help you apply your coaching skills in the workplace. We'll explore the different ways you can use coaching as you get on with the job in hand: whether that's in formal, planned coaching sessions, or coaching 'on the hoof', as a natural response to everyday exchanges with your colleagues. Of course, your coaching needs to get as good and preferably better results than you're used to before you'll adopt it in practice. So, you'll find fresh perspectives on familiar situations, where coaching principles really work. I'll show you how you can adopt a quick coaching response to create progress on a task or issue, while you also help someone to think and learn for themselves.

Part 4: Action - how can you take your learning forward?

The final part helps you to consider what you can do next, to build stronger coaching ability going forward. We'll look at simple ideas to maintain your focus on coaching and sustain the momentum you've gained through reading the book. As you might imagine, to help you integrate coaching behaviour in your workplace, I'll use coaching questions. You will be encouraged to reflect on your immediate opportunities to coach or explore what might still block your way. As you prepare for the road ahead, you'll be ready to spot opportunities, tackle issues and apply the ideas in this book to make a positive difference to your workplace.

Reader toolkit

Along the way, you'll also notice bite-sized inserts intended to support your practice and learning. This is your toolkit, and it consists of the following:

Pause and reflect

These are questions to help coach your own learning and link ideas to your own situation. You can choose to write your answers down, speak them out loud, or just pause and think them through. The important thing to remember is that the questions are intended to provoke you to think and act, just like a coach does in a coaching conversation. So, by focusing on your responses to these questions, you're letting the book go to work for you.

Ideas to action

These exercises deepen your understanding and ability by applying principles or behaviours to real life. You'll be asked to try something out, often in an everyday situation, such as a conversation or meeting. Please take the time to try some of these, as only in the 'doing' will you really reap the benefits of some of the powerful ideas on offer.

At a glance

Here you'll find handy hints or advice to help you to get to grips with the key points of a situation – for example, the main dos and don'ts of giving effective feedback, or what to avoid when agreeing on actions or next steps. Like the rest of the toolkit, the tips form a quick visual reminder that you can reference afterwards.

Checklists

The checklists will remind you of key points or principles, at a useful point in your reading. They will help you to plan for a situation and make sure that you're feeling prepared and well-equipped – for example when tackling a tough conversation or preparing to run a meeting according to coaching principles. By thinking and preparing a little in advance, you can save headaches later.

 **Definitions**

In these boxes, jargon is busted, and buzzwords foiled, as you find clear and concise meanings to commonly used terms, for example, the difference between coaching and mentoring, or what we mean by the term 'facilitation'. Often all that's needed is to confirm what you already suspected! I hope you'll be heartened by how much you already know.

 Self-awareness Check

Much of our ability to change our behaviour begins with an increase in our self-awareness and so in these boxes, you will be encouraged to consider your current attitudes, behaviours or beliefs, in order to increase your self-awareness (and so choices).

 In a nutshell

I'll end most chapters with a summary so you can confirm what we've covered or remind yourself of key points to focus on. These boxes also serve as a quick list to help you recap a topic at speed when you want to.

Decide your reading approach

This book can be read from front to back, in full or in part, or you may choose to cherry-pick from key ideas that most interest you. Maybe you want to read lists of effective coaching questions or gain a fresh perspective on listening. Or perhaps you tend to avoid giving feedback and want to find comfortable ways of doing that. Whatever your preferred approach is, I aim to support you with your current challenges and goals. So, without delay, let's look first at what coaching is, and why it's such a great skill for you to have in the workplace.

PART 1

Awareness

CHAPTER 1

What is coaching?

This chapter will explain what coaching is, how it works, and – importantly – how it can work for you. I'll explain the differences in a coaching conversation plus the benefits that adopting a coaching style can bring. We'll look at the difference between directive and less directive styles of influence. You'll then be asked to reflect on your own influencing style, to highlight your opportunities to improve right now.

What is coaching at work?

As a practical activity, coaching is a style of conversation, or conversations, that one person has with another. The person who is the coach wants to create a conversation that will benefit the other person, for example their learning, action and results. Coaching conversations can happen in different environments and over different timeframes. For example, you might coach someone during a quick chat at the coffee machine or in a more formal meeting where you need to discuss something at length.

Whether an exchange is a coaching conversation (or not) is more about the style of the conversation than its location, length or content. A coaching conversation might last two minutes or two hours since, ultimately, coaching is defined by its impact. Consider this example: I might lecture someone for an hour on what I think they should do in a situation, and they may rightfully choose to ignore me. Or I may ask a simple yet challenging question, such as 'What do you think's really holding you back here?' This may make them realise something that previously lay hidden. The second example has more of a coaching effect because it causes the person to think and, therefore, come to their own conclusion.

The following questions can help you spot if a conversation might be called coaching:

● Is the focus of the conversation mostly on the individual being coached?

● Is the intention of the coach positive towards the person being coached?

● Is the coach using skills of listening, questioning and reflection?

● Will the individual think about the conversation afterwards and benefit from that reflection?

● Does the conversation benefit the thinking, learning or actions of someone in some way?

 Pause and reflect

What are your opportunities to coach?

Use the following questions to identify the potential benefit of coaching for you:

Ⓠ How often do people ask you questions about their work and expect you to give them solutions or advice? For example, 'How do I do this?' or 'This has happened – what shall I do?'

Ⓠ How 'indispensable' do you feel at work? Would things fall to pieces if you weren't there to look after everyone?

Ⓠ If someone comes to you with a problem, do you help them by giving them your thoughts, or do you encourage them to voice theirs?

If it helps, get someone you trust to reflect on your answers. You never know, you might be coaching more often than you imagine.

Coaching is often catalytic in its impact, for example as it provokes deeper thought or appreciation of a topic. Whether the person being coached would have had those thoughts, insights or ideas without that conversation having happened is often best decided by them. So, the best judge of whether a conversation had a coaching effect is the person being coached, rather than the person trying to coach them.

Why does coaching at work, work?

Effective coaching increases the *performance* of people. It also engages people, by challenging them to think, act and ultimately learn for themselves. As a manager or leader, it is not enough to be a talented or expert individual. To create lasting results, managers must be able to develop the talent and output of people as a consistent outcome. However, it serves no one if how they get results is by being overly controlling, or micromanaging, or if they create high levels of stress or overwhelm as they do so. Instead, a manager must be able to bring out the best in individuals, sometimes by relaxing the amount of control exerted upon them. As a coaching manager, during a conversation, you focus on the person as well as the task or situation being discussed. That means you can emphasise the ability of the person to take a situation forward, rather than fixing the situation for yourself. That can feel uncomfortable at first and you need to know which simple responses will equip you to do that. In Chapter 8, The Steppingstones Model shows you different ways to exert more or less control during a conversation.

> Managers who coach listen a little more closely, ask a few more questions and encourage others to think and act for themselves

Managers who coach listen a little more closely, ask a few more questions and encourage others to think and act for themselves. By using these simple behaviours, you help others to stay effective, plus empower them by encouraging them to learn for themselves. A bit like teaching a hungry man to fish, it's a sustainable solution.

Definitions

Direct report

Someone who reports to you directly, that is there is no other manager or supervisor between you on a reporting line or structure chart.

Subordinate

Someone who is less senior to you in the organisation; they have a less responsible role or lower-graded position, and so on. In this book, the term is used to mean the same as a direct report (above).

Colleague

Anyone you work with, including direct reports, subordinates, or people senior to you within the organisation.

Team member

I use this term to indicate a member of a team that reports to you. This assumes that you are managing a team; if you're not, that's fine, simply imagine that you are. Logically, the team members we'll discuss are also your direct reports, subordinates, and colleagues.

Peer

This is someone on the same level as you; their role is regarded as equivalent to your role in terms of its responsibility, grade, place in the hierarchy, and so on. Remember that while we consider all *people* equal, we acknowledge that sometimes the *roles* they perform are judged to have greater or lesser value within organisations, often because of the responsibility or impact of the role.

How does coaching at work, work?

Coaching ideas and behaviours work in a broad range of situations and interactions, for example:

- Face-to-face conversations, planned and unplanned, formal and informal

- In group and 1:1 conversation
- In an online meeting situation, for example over Zoom, Teams and so on.
- In email exchanges
- Over the telephone

When we coach someone, we assume that, with encouragement, they can work things out for themselves. So, we ask questions like 'What are your options?' or 'So, what needs to happen?' or 'What do you want to do?' That simple shift, from giving advice to asking someone what they are going to do, is at the heart of coaching as a management style.

To coach effectively we make an effort to become better listeners, and to build our ability to enquire and understand the views and ideas of someone else. In conversation, we also make building openness and trust important, as a basis of our influence. We'll focus on these skills (and others) directly in the ability/skills section.

Engagement beats compliance

One of the benefits of adopting a less directive (less 'tell') coaching posture in conversation is that when people work things out for themselves, they are more engaged in the solution. Conversely, if we tell someone to do something, and it doesn't work out, they might feel less responsibility for its failure. For example, I tell Janis to get everyone who is involved in a work issue

> When people work things out for themselves, they are more engaged in the solution

together for a meeting, so that we can agree on a solution. But when Janis tries to arrange the meeting, it's tough to get everyone together on the same day. If it's not Janis's idea in the first place, he's less likely to look for ways to turn the situation around. On the other hand, if it was Janis who suggested the meeting, he'll be reluctant to come back with the news of its failure. Instead, he is going to look for ways to overcome potential barriers, rather than deliver the news, 'It's not possible – everyone's too busy.'

Also, when you encourage people to be more responsible, gradually their confidence increases – and so does their sense of empowerment (their ability to act). As you stop automatically helping or rescuing people, you empower them.

Virtual teams and an increase in remote working

Our modern workplace sees managers and leaders challenged to manage teams based in far-reaching geographic locations and/or working from home. This has resulted in an increase in video conference meetings via Microsoft Teams, Zoom, and so on. The challenges of remote teams and home working include:

- How to sustain clarity of communication/mutual understanding?
- How to retain a focus on priorities, productivity and so on?
- How to maintain people's sense of affinity to the organisation?

In these situations, the skills of coaching are an invaluable resource as managers learn to facilitate a conversation, rather than dominate it. When using coaching ideas, the manager typically talks less, listens more and engages the other people to contribute their thoughts and views. Imagine a team meeting via video conference where the manager is involving every member on screen, for example by asking them questions, demonstrating that they have been heard and facilitating enquiry to create mutual understanding and clarity. Now imagine the same manager doing all the talking and filling in embarrassing silences, while people simply sit and watch. This non-coaching posture encourages people to disengage, contribute less, and potentially feel disconnected from the conversation and/or team. Coaching skills support the virtual workplace as effectively as in a traditional, shared workspace and play a valuable role in meeting contemporary challenges.

Directed or self-directed – what's the difference?

Coaching in the workplace means that you adopt a less directive style of influencing or managing others. Literally, this means that you choose to give less advice and fewer answers. Instead, you trust that people often know what they need to and can direct themselves pretty well. By using some simple ideas and behaviours (such as, 'talk less and listen more'), you can encourage people to form their own thoughts and views about a situation.

This shift of your emphasis can happen in any exchange, for example, a face-to-face conversation, during a Zoom or Teams meeting, or even over an email dialogue. The simple, critical shift is that when you coach someone, you encourage them to be self-directed. This demands that you are willing to operate from a different set of principles. For example, instead of 'I know how', sometimes you choose to trust that 'they know how'. Figure 1.1 illustrates these two different ways of everyday influence.

Directive	Self-directed
• I know how	• You know how
• I tell you	• I ask you
• You follow instruction	• You decide

Figure 1.1 Spectrum of influence

The following uses the same situation to show how a manager responds to a subordinate, using these two different styles of influence.

Manager is directive	Manager encourages self-direction
You need to phone Carla and get her involved in this.	Okay, right, I understand, so what do you need to do?
I reckon this is another issue with planning again; we're just not able to estimate timescales accurately.	This is a fairly frequent issue, isn't it? What do you think is causing it?
Well, I'd suggest not releasing the information for a week. Let people get used to the idea.	Okay, what's the best plan to communicate this, do you think?

You don't have to be nice to coach

You'll notice in the above examples that both styles have no dependency on tone or niceness. Indeed, it's possible to be really 'nice' and *highly directive*. For example:

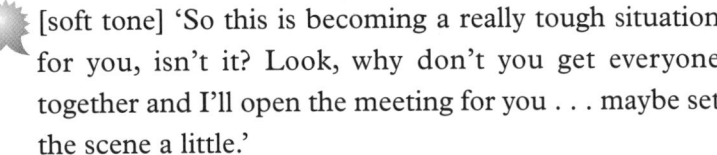

[soft tone] 'So this is becoming a really tough situation for you, isn't it? Look, why don't you get everyone together and I'll open the meeting for you . . . maybe set the scene a little.'

Here the manager was obviously being nice, warm, supportive – and highly directive. They've just given an instruction, based on an assumption that they know best. Also, since the manager has stepped in to help, a subtle shift of responsibility for the issue has taken place. They've offered to rescue the subordinate and therefore potentially made them feel like a victim. The meeting may be a great idea; it's simply that the subordinate wasn't involved in thinking things through or coming up with a plan. That's what makes the manager's style directive.

Self-awareness check

Q. Are you cynical about coaching?

If you're a little sceptical about coaching, I welcome your reservations.
Quite often your doubt is simply a signal to find something true for
you. My task is not to convince you of something I think is true, but to
help you reveal *your* truth about yourself and how you collaborate
with people. It's up to you to decide which thoughts or ideas in this
book will work for you. Once you've discovered something for yourself,
it becomes *yours*, not mine, or anyone else's.

Coaching is not by definition 'nice' or 'soft' – it can be very challenging. A manager can influence others in a less directive way
while being pretty punchy. For example:

[strong tone] 'Yes, right, so I totally understand what
you're saying, I just need to know what you've decided
to do . . .'

Here the manager acknowledges they've heard what's happening
and is challenging the subordinate to come up with an answer.

You might not like the mildly aggres-
sive tone, but that's not the point.
The thing to notice is that this manager is encouraging, or maybe even
forcing, a subordinate to 'own' both
the situation and its solution. That's
what makes it less directive as a style

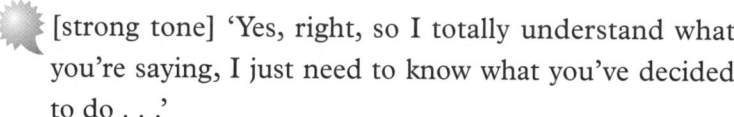

Sometimes a less directive
style can put a subordinate
under more pressure in a
situation

of influence. As they are placed in a clearer position of responsibility, sometimes a less directive style can put a subordinate under
more pressure in a situation. As a manager, your role is to judge
whether that is a constructive and helpful thing to do for them.

Tough guy or teddy bear? – As a coach, you can be either

How much warmth is needed depends on the person and the situation; ultimately you will decide for yourself. But let's be clear that while coaching can be warm, encouraging and friendly, it isn't defined by those terms. What's more important is that the person you are coaching is engaged in the conversation with you. Some people are actually turned off by a friendly style and would prefer straight talking. Only you can judge what will work best for you with the people or situations you experience. However, it's important to develop flexibility with the different styles, as this enables you to adapt to different people and situations in a variety of ways. We'll deal with this topic more directly in the skills outlined in Part 2.

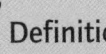

Definition

How is a mentor different from a coach?

In the workplace, a mentor intends to provide you with overarching support for your situations, including your general career development. Traditionally, a mentor is thought of as a 'wise guide' because of their relevant skills or knowledge. In the workplace, a mentor is likely to tell stories and offer opinions or advice as their professional experience is relevant to your situation. Where it appears appropriate (and if they are willing), they may even provide tangible assistance. While they may have great communication skills, such as those covered in this book, these skills are not required for them to be effective. The unique difference of a mentor is in the intentions of the relationship. For example, their influence often comes from an exchange of benevolence and respect, that is they feel benevolent towards you and you have developed a respect for them.

While mentoring might appear to be a more 'directive' activity, good mentors often have coaching skills, because without the ability to listen, question and offer challenges or feedback, a mentor's advice may be irrelevant or unwelcome.

For a fuller appreciation of this unique role, see my book *The Mentoring Manual* (Pearson 2021).

When being directive 'works'

There's nothing wrong with being directive and sometimes it's the best approach; for example, you can't coach knowledge. Here's when trying to have someone think or decide for themselves is less helpful:

> You can't coach knowledge

- When someone has no information or experience to draw upon to solve their issue, for example maybe they need to know where to find a piece of data. There are many options, you know where that is and so it's pointless to ask them where they might find it.

- When asking someone to decide for themselves is not possible, for example there's a standard process they need to follow, to adhere to regulations.

- When someone is anxious or under pressure, and to ask them to analyse or decide something will increase that pressure. When we are anxious, we're less able to think clearly, and what we need is reassurance and guidance, rather than more pressure. If you ask someone who's feeling anxious a list of challenging questions, that won't help – although asking a question that helps them to calm down might.

At a glance

Stay aware, stop telling and start asking

Coaching can be a quick and simple adjustment. For example, when someone explains a problem to you, instead of responding with, 'Okay, here's what you need to do ...', simply ask them, 'Okay, so what do you think needs to happen?' To make the switch you first need to catch your automatic response, so stay aware!

When being directive works less well

Being constantly directive is an inflexible style that creates pitfalls for a manager over time. People who are always told what to do don't learn effectively, and potentially become bored, lacklustre or demotivated. Since they are not encouraged to think, they may also become dependent or even lazy, for example ask their manager for frequent, or basic, instruction. As people's sense of empowerment reduces, they become hesitant or lack the confidence to act. They follow direct instructions but might not be as engaged in their manager's solutions as they could be, for example 'Well, I'll do it because you've told me to, but it's not going to work'.

Another consequence of an overly directive manager is that their team aren't stimulated to think for themselves and so their own creativity or thinking processes are dulled. Solving problems becomes something the manager does, so why bother thinking about what the solutions might be?

Figure 1.2 illustrates how the directive and self-directed styles impact relationships and responses over time.

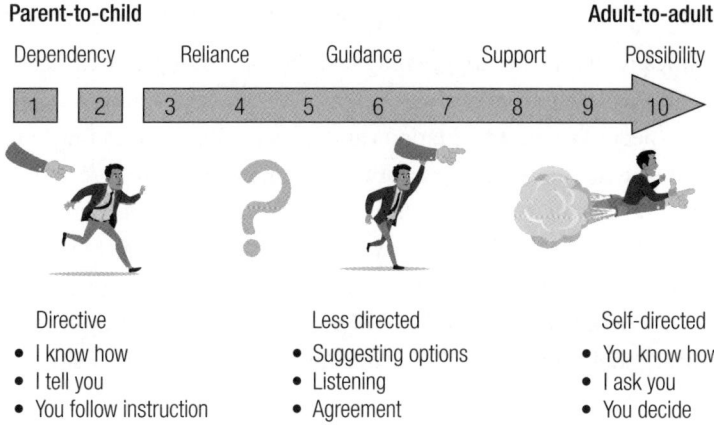

Figure 1.2 Scale of influence

When you parent people they might act like children

A manager can complain 'Why can't my team think for themselves?', yet the source of their people's dependency upon them is actually the manager. When a manager is frequently directive, the dynamic of their relationships with people who work for them can feel like 'parent-to-child'. As they give detailed instructions and solutions instead of encouraging someone to work things out for themselves, the manager 'parents' their team. Over time, this 'parenting' means people learn to expect instructions and solutions – and so become dependent on that. Over time, how you manage and influence affects the nature of your relationship with your team and how they develop and grow.

> How you manage and influence affects the nature of your relationship with your team and how they develop and grow

Helping others can create overwhelm for a manager

Ironically, while a manager may feel they are trying to help their team, they actually create an unhelpful downward spiral. As they are expected to direct situations and have all the answers for their team, the demands and pressure on the manager's own workload increase. As their time is taken up by the people who report to them, the managers have less available time to focus on their own tasks. When managers let go of this type of micro-managing, they can contribute a different level of involvement, for example supporting their own manager, or deciding priorities/strategy for the whole team.

When a manager encourages a subordinate to think, act and learn for themselves, the relationship feels more like 'adult-to-adult'. Over time, subordinates learn to expect to be challenged by questions such as 'What's the real issue we need to solve here?' or 'What do you suggest then?' As they predict the manager's coaching response, they come prepared with opinions, ideas and suggestions more often. Over time, they'll feel an increased sense of engagement and ownership of their own situations as well.

Self-awareness check

How directive are you?

Use the questions below to assess how often you coach and how often you direct, or 'tell'. Then perhaps return to these questions once you've worked more with this subject, for example after you've finished this book.

Q How often do you give specific, direct instruction to people who work for you?

Q When people are explaining issues, challenges, or difficulties, how much do you listen and question – and how much do you talk?

Q How often do you automatically offer ideas or advice to the people you work with?

Q If someone tells you about a problem, do you immediately try to solve it?

Q Does it ever feel as though you are 'parenting' your team?

Based on your answers to the above, rate your own style of influence, using the 1–0 scale in Figure 1.2. Now get someone you know and trust to give their view of your typical style. Finally, look for opportunities to improve your scores, perhaps through discussion with the same person.

In a nutshell

What is coaching?

Coaching is a less directive style of conversation that encourages people to think and decide for themselves. An effective coach uses heightened levels of key skills such as listening, questioning, reflection and feedback. When managers coach people effectively, they create a positive impact on their performance, engagement and on their ongoing development. The benefits for managers include freeing up the time they waste managing detail that others are capable of handling, which enables them to focus more strategically or creatively over time.

For anyone who wants to increase their ability to influence in conversation, coaching enables just that. For any manager in the workplace, the ability to coach others is a core competence.

CHAPTER 2

Coaching as an enabler of engagement

In this chapter, we'll look at the critical link between the principles of coaching and your ability to engage and motivate people in the workplace. Whether you work in a small business or a large organisation, engagement levels affect people's behaviour around you every day. To confirm your awareness, I'll offer simple definitions of engagement and help you consider its relevance to you. Using questions and prompts, I'll also help you decide where you might benefit from a sharper focus on this fascinating topic. Finally, we'll explore what you can do in conversation to increase someone's engagement level.

Of course, if you are super-keen to learn about coaching more directly, simply scan this section and skip to the next chapter.

What do we mean by engagement?

Engagement relates to our sense of connection, value and motivation around a task or situation. At work, it's the difference between people doing what they need to do and going beyond what was expected of them. There are many industry definitions, and here are three simple examples:

'Engaged employees are those who are involved in, enthusiastic about and committed to their work and workplace,' Gallup

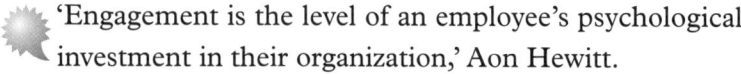 'Engagement is the level of an employee's psychological investment in their organization,' Aon Hewitt.

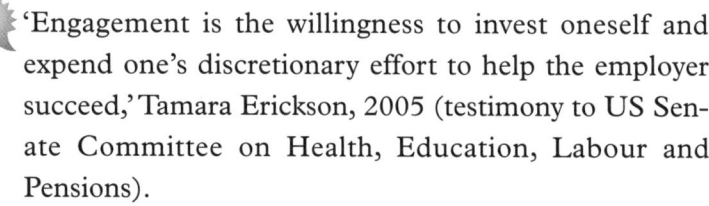 'Engagement is the willingness to invest oneself and expend one's discretionary effort to help the employer succeed,' Tamara Erickson, 2005 (testimony to US Senate Committee on Health, Education, Labour and Pensions).

Why is engagement important in the workplace?

Organisations now realise that for businesses to thrive, first people must thrive

The recent surge of interest, research and focus on this topic is logical and positive; organisations now realise that for businesses to thrive, first people must thrive.

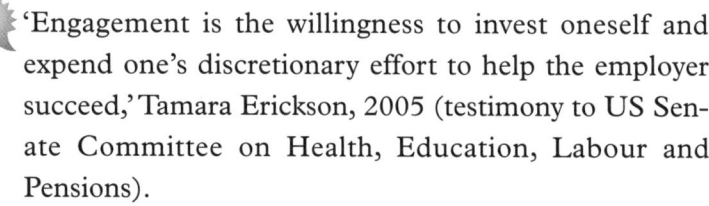 'Companies with high (and sustainable) levels of engagement had an average one-year operating margin almost three times higher than those with lower levels of engagement.'

Towers Watson, (formerly Towers Perrin Consulting) 2012

Clearly, this is a high-value topic, and your ability to engage your colleagues can mean a dramatic increase in your results. In quality and service terms, the difference between those who are engaged and those who are not is tangible, because our engagement level shapes our attitude and our actions, for example:

- In a store, if you ask an assistant where you might find a product, do they point in the vague direction of the aisle, or do they take you to it?

- When you're on a call to a service centre and your mobile phone signal drops, does the operator phone you back, or simply move on to their next call?

- If one of your team notices that a customer has left something behind, what do they do?

What does this have to do with you?

Your style and approach to how you manage others impact how people think, how they feel and what they do – which affects their engagement levels. Also, to inspire and motivate others, you need their engagement. How responsive are they to your requests? Do they do what they say they will do? In a crisis, can you rely on their goodwill? Here are just a few ways that you impact people's engagement levels directly:

- Your attitude towards people, for example the respect and value that you demonstrate
- The clarity you create for people around vision, objectives and priorities
- The sense of purpose that you encourage, for example by what you make important
- How much you challenge and support others to learn and progress
- Whether they trust you to act in their best interests, for example, that you want what is positive for them.

It's important to acknowledge that some factors of engagement might be beyond your control, such as the trading environment or people's basic wellness. However, as a manager, you do hold the keys to many of them. This is, of course, a good and positive thing as it enables you to make a worthwhile contribution personally and professionally.

'Managers who are able to create an all-around engaging work climate can have an invaluable effect on an employee's commitment to an organisation and the productivity a group of employees can generate.'

Mel Stark, Hay Group

How does coaching link to engagement?

At a basic level, if someone is not engaged in a conversation with you, they are less likely to be open to you coaching them. As you move away from a more directive style (where you talk and they listen), you now rely on someone to participate more fully in a conversation. This is because you want someone to actively involve themselves in the conversation, make an effort to think things through, offer ideas, and so on. Having a simple understanding of what engagement is can help with that.

The real opportunity of coaching behaviours, however, is to increase people's engagement levels more broadly in relation to how they perform at work. Let's now focus on that opportunity directly.

What drives our engagement?

As you'd expect, what engages people is both common and individual, for example, we all like a healthy level of challenge and we all enjoy a positive sense of learning and progress. However, some of us are enlivened by receiving praise, while others just want to see results. Our sense of engagement involves our head *and* our heart; just because we may logically know we should do something does not instantly make us joyful at the prospect of that. Coaching conversations enable you to learn what someone's individual drivers are, as you'll see later in this section.

> Our sense of engagement involves our head *and* our heart

There is now a huge effort to evidence and understand the common (and core) drivers of engagement. For example, a UK government-sponsored study (the MacCleod Review/Employee Engagement Task Force 2008–2012) lists the top drivers of employee engagement as:

1   Visible, empowering leadership with a strong strategic organisational narrative, for example, where the organisation has come from and where it's going to.

2 Engaging managers who:

- focus on their people and give them scope to act
- treat their people as individuals, and
- coach and stretch their people.

3 Employees having a voice throughout the organisation, to reinforce and challenge views. Employees are seen as central to 'the solution'.

As a leader or manager, you have a direct or indirect influence on all the above. For example, when you adopt a coaching style in conversation you can influence:

- people's alignment with company purpose and objectives, for example by using questions such as 'How does this situation relate to our drive for innovation?'
- their learning, growth and empowerment, for example as you build their confidence to think and act for themselves
- people's sense of being positively challenged, for example by not always fixing things for them, or by offering regular and constructive feedback
- how valued people feel – because you listen to them, ask them what they think and encourage them to act on their own ideas
- their experience of organisational values, such as openness and respect; for example, 'What are your views on this?' or 'What do you think needs to happen here?'

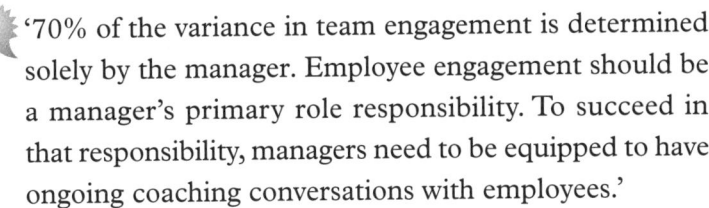

'70% of the variance in team engagement is determined solely by the manager. Employee engagement should be a manager's primary role responsibility. To succeed in that responsibility, managers need to be equipped to have ongoing coaching conversations with employees.'

Gallup.com

Pause and reflect

How well do you engage others?

Use the following questions to assess how effective you are at engaging, motivating and inspiring others.

With your team

Q How engaged does your team appear (individually/as a group)? For example, if you aren't there, or don't check in, what happens to productivity?

Q How aligned is your team behind a sense of purpose? For example, do they have a shared view of what's important?

Q How effectively do you maintain people's clarity about what needs to be done?

Q When you give someone a task or project, how do they respond? Do they get behind your initiatives and deliver? Or do they go into hiding, or deliver something 'half-done'?

Q How much do you focus on and support people's overall well-being?

With colleagues

Q How often do you consider people as individuals? For example, what's important to them, what their preferences are, and so on.

Q In conversation, do you flex your style to individuals? For example, this person welcomes detail, this person enjoys optimism, and so on.

Q How much do people enjoy and value working with you?

Please stay positive, look for simple ideas for sustainable improvement, and keep those achievable. Trying to become an engagement superhero overnight is likely to be counter-productive, simply because you risk being overwhelmed by doing that. If it helps, ask the opinion of someone you trust for ideas or insights.

Coaching conversations enable engagement

Clearly, coaching is a style of conversation that places greater emphasis and importance upon the person you are coaching (rather than simply the task to get done). The table below illustrates more fully how the key drivers of engagement are naturally supported by coaching.

Coaching behaviour/principle	Link to engagement
Active listening, e.g. seeking first to understand	Helps people feel valued, promotes openness and trust
Active enquiry, e.g. use of open questions	Challenges people to think and express themselves more clearly
Facilitating the thoughts of another, e.g. what needs to happen first?	Demonstrates that their ideas and views are relevant and valuable
Encourage someone to think and act for themselves, e.g. what's possible? Or what can you do?	Affirms responsibility, ownership, and empowerment Accelerates learning and development Encourages resourcefulness and resilience Creates 'adult–adult' relationships with subordinates
Offer challenge, observations and constructive feedback	Challenges the individual, promotes a high-performance culture, develops talent
Assume that other people can do more, be more	Creates a filter for 'possibility' Plus, you naturally emphasise the value of the people who work for you (and promote high esteem)

▶

Coaching behaviour/principle	Link to engagement
Increase your focus on the need to develop others, e.g. 'I need to create the context in which others are successful'	Builds someone's awareness of their own potential in a practical way Accelerates learning As you increase your utilisation of people, you also realise their potential more fully
We work from a paradigm of interdependency, e.g. we create results through others	Challenges the individual to do more, be more (and so increases enjoyment) Strengthens communities (teams), as you focus on the capacity of the whole team as a practical extension of yourself

Engaged managers engage people

To engage others around a topic or task, your own engagement levels must also be positive. So, it's useful to consider your own engagement from time to time. In this way, you can increase your enjoyment and contribution, while learning what is likely to engage people around you. For example, are you reading this book because you want to? Or because you feel that you should? Maybe your engagement level falls somewhere between those two ideas, that is you feel you should but also you are beginning to realise that you'll benefit from doing so.

At work more generally, you will have activities that you happily arrive early for, and some that you put off and avoid. When we ask ourselves why this is, the answer isn't always simple. For example, you might volunteer to do something, because you feel it's important and something that you're able to do, but then when the time arrives to start the task you procrastinate.

To understand what causes or inhibits engagement (in yourself or others) it's useful to view engagement as having component parts:

The intellectual part How we understand something, how clear we are about it and what our view/opinion is of that

The emotional part How we feel about doing something; the emotions that are being created by our thoughts/ understanding

The enabling/'in action' part What we are doing (the actions we are taking) in response to our understanding, views and feelings about something

Towers Watson (formerly Towers Perrin Consulting)

It's possible to coach yourself (and others) on these three topics, by enquiring into them more directly. To experience this yourself, use the questions below.

Self-awareness check

How engaged are you in a situation?

Think of a task or activity that you would like to make better progress in, or a situation that you know you avoid tackling. Use the following list to explore your engagement around that more fully. As you reflect on the questions, it helps to handwrite simple notes to capture your thoughts.

The intellectual part: understanding

(Q) How clear are you about what you need to do in this situation?

(Q) What don't you know, or are unclear about?

(Q) What are your simple steps forward? What are the immediate priorities?

▶

The emotional part: affinity

Q What is your personal sense of connection (affinity) to this situation or task? For example, how do you feel about it?

Q What's your own reason for doing it? For example, how might you benefit? Or what's important about this for you?

Q When you imagine this task or situation, how enlivened do you feel by that?

The enabling part: in motion

Q How 'in action' are you around this situation? What have you done to make progress?

Q What are your potential blocks or barriers to action? What's stopping you?

Q How clearly are you focused on the priorities and on actions that will make the most difference?

Go back over your notes and highlight any insights or actions needed to increase your engagement. If it helps, discuss the situation with someone you trust to support you.

Build your own engagement and then coach it in others

Once you're familiar with the three-part structure and typical questions shown in the box above, you can use those to increase the engagement of others – for example when your team member or colleague doesn't seem to be making progress in a situation, or when you've given a task to someone, they aren't making effective progress, and you don't fully understand why.

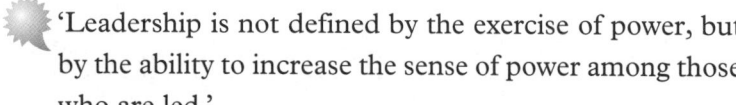 'Leadership is not defined by the exercise of power, but by the ability to increase the sense of power among those who are led.'

Mary Parker Follett, *Creative Leadership*, 1924

Transactional engagement, burnout and coaching

Sometimes people act/appear engaged, but their engagement is unsustainable over time; this is known as transactional engagement. For example, in an openly competitive workplace people often work longer and harder because that's what's expected of them – for example 'I need to look engaged here'. Some people believe that they need to demonstrate a commitment to the company that goes beyond considerations of themselves. Perhaps career development opportunities are scarce, or the threat of redundancy is regular. Unfortunately, when we do not recover or recharge from working at peak levels, our resilience and enjoyment wane. Where extreme stress becomes permanent rather than temporary, people's productivity suffers over time. Ultimately people whose engagement is transactional might burn out or choose to leave an organisation to redress their work-life balance or because the situation has become unsustainable for them personally.

> Where extreme stress becomes permanent rather than temporary, people's productivity suffers over time

Effective coaching conversations reduce the negative element of transactional engagement. Here's why:

- As you listen more and ask better questions, you improve your relationships and people are more open with you about what they really think and feel.

- Your awareness of people's views, attitudes and motivation broadens and deepens.

- When people aren't coping as well as they may appear, you are in a better position to support them – for example by helping them share their true feelings, readjust priorities, and set helpful boundaries around their work.

At a glance

Engage someone in conversation

To increase someone's levels of engagement around a situation or task, remember that they need:

● to be clear about what needs to be done

● to feel a positive personal connection to that in some way, for example, that what they are doing seems worthwhile/they can see a positive

● to be in tangible action towards that (and be enabled to act).

During the conversation, try one or more of the following:

● Ask more questions, let them speak, for example 'what do you think will work here?'

● Show sincere interest in them/their views, for example, use appropriate body postures and eye contact.

● Summarise occasionally – indicate your effort to listen to and understand them.

● Focus on the components and blockers to engagement – see the earlier Pause and reflect box, 'How engaged are you in a situation?'

● Be willing to talk about what they are less happy about; for example, make it okay for them to be less than positive or share their concerns.

As we decide to coach engagement, each person, group, and situation presents fresh challenges. However, once you develop your awareness of engagement, and the underlying causes or blocks to that, you can make progress where less aware managers cannot.

Engaging people is personal

When you explore the personal aspects of people's performance, this can reveal how they truly think and feel, and you may be less comfortable with that. For example, you've asked someone to create a report on store trading figures. You've chased them already; it's been weeks and they still haven't begun the task.

This is where a directive style of managing people (I instruct, you comply) often seems preferable. After all, if you keep conversations to the bare facts and logic ('I need you to do this by the end of Friday please'), isn't everything simple and easy? The answer is, of course, sometimes, for a while, and not always. Much of the cause of how disengaged people feel at work arises from a lack of focus on people's basic human qualities, that is we are both logical and emotional beings. We have basic hopes, desires, feelings and needs which must also be considered alongside business goals. In this case, a less directive style might ask 'What's stopping you from getting started here?', which means you need to hear whatever that might be. Perhaps they tell you that they don't enjoy creating reports, for example 'I dread going through all the store spreadsheets; I get really stressed at the idea of it'.

Perhaps you're comfortable helping people realise what needs doing (intellectual) and also the steps towards that (action) but typically you might skip the middle component of engagement, which is how they feel about it (personal connection/affinity). That's understandable and yet a false barrier to your ability to create results through other people. A coaching style helps you to do this naturally as you learn to attune more closely to individuals in conversation. Also, because of the principles and structure underneath those, it offers you a more predictable and comfortable way to do that. For illustrations of structured conversations, see Part 3 ('Application').

In a nutshell

In the challenge to engage people, coaching is a critical link

When people are engaged, they are naturally enlivened and motivated to do a great job. They enjoy their work and the challenge and learning that it provides them. Surveys consistently prove that this is good for quality, customers and bottom-line performance.

The things that engage us are both common and individual. For example, we all enjoy a worthwhile challenge and clear sense of purpose. In addition, we have individual preferences; for example you enjoy an ambitious challenge while I might not. Coaching behaviours help to increase people's engagement as they support many of the factors that affect that, that is someone's understanding, affinity and action. For example, by using behaviours such as listening and asking great questions, you reveal what someone enjoys and responds to as an individual.

CHAPTER 3

What is the mindset of a coaching manager?

I n this chapter, we'll look at the supporting values and beliefs that drive your management style and behaviour. I'll encourage you to reflect on what you believe it means to be a manager, because knowing what style of manager you currently are, and what kind of manager you'd like to be, will help you develop. We'll look at traditional, directive models of management alongside the values that support a coaching style of manager.

First, let's look at how you think you add value as a manager. For example, if you believe 'My team value my experience and my ability to give them expert advice', then that's going to encourage you to always offer ideas and solutions. Or if you think that being a manager means helping your team to be individually successful, then your actions will reflect that. When we decide to operate from different principles or develop new skills, we first need to know what our typical tendencies are, so we can notice them in action. This everyday self-awareness offers the chance to change and grow.

> Self-awareness offers the chance to change and grow

What beliefs cause us to be a highly directive manager?

A subtle pressure goes with being the most senior person in the team, and that pressure is that you are expected to know everything or at least the 'right' thing. After all, they made you the manager, didn't they? However, even when you do have all the answers, sometimes you add more value to your team when you encourage them to find those, or different, answers on their own.

Let's look at the basic assumptions a directive manager might have and how they may act because of those. Figure 3.1 illustrates the values and beliefs of a highly directive manager and predicts the skills and behaviours that develop.

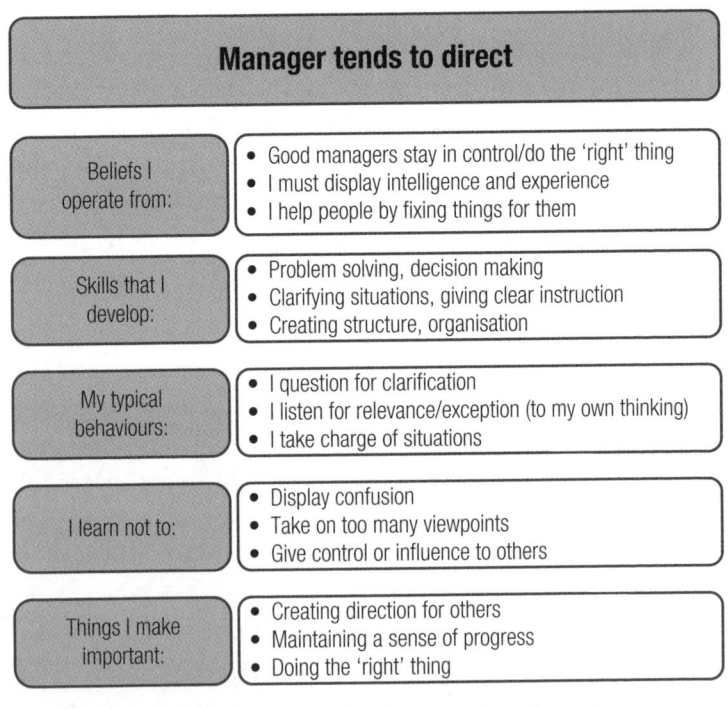

Manager tends to direct

| Beliefs I operate from: | • Good managers stay in control/do the 'right' thing
• I must display intelligence and experience
• I help people by fixing things for them |

| Skills that I develop: | • Problem solving, decision making
• Clarifying situations, giving clear instruction
• Creating structure, organisation |

| My typical behaviours: | • I question for clarification
• I listen for relevance/exception (to my own thinking)
• I take charge of situations |

| I learn not to: | • Display confusion
• Take on too many viewpoints
• Give control or influence to others |

| Things I make important: | • Creating direction for others
• Maintaining a sense of progress
• Doing the 'right' thing |

Figure 3.1 Values, beliefs and behaviours of a directive manager

This directive mindset is not bad or wrong; there are times when this mindset creates positive leadership. Sometimes simple direction and instruction give people the confidence and clarity that are needed. In the armed forces, a directive model suits many situations, including combat. Interestingly, both the US and UK military have tangible interest and activity in coaching and mentoring styles of leadership. This is because, over time, sole reliance on the directive model exposes pitfalls. These pitfalls include:

- The leader/manager puts themselves under pressure to know everything and 'be right' all the time.

- The team assume that the leader/manager wants to be involved and 'give answers', which takes more of the manager's time and can result in a 'fire-fighting' type of role for the manager.

- In their tendency to rely on the leader/manager, the team appear lazy, demotivated or lacking in confidence, which causes frustration for the manager; for example, 'I sometimes feel like I'm a nursemaid'.

Definition

Facilitation

To facilitate a conversation is to help guide it through to a logical completion. A facilitator is focused more on the process of the conversation than the content of it: their role is to guide an individual or group through the planned stages of the conversation. In a pure facilitation role, you do not contribute any content to the discussion yourself, you simply encourage the group to stay focused, keep the discussion relevant, close down or open up a conversation, keep time, and so on. Your priority is to make the session effective by supporting others to think something through effectively.

What beliefs help you to be a coaching manager?

Managers who adopt a more consistent coaching style operate from a distinct set of assumptions or beliefs. These beliefs enable them to relax the pressures to know everything or to control and direct every situation. A coaching manager places value on people's ability to think and act for themselves, and upon their own need to create conditions in which their team will be successful.

Your beliefs affect your sense of priority, on an everyday basis. For example, as a coaching manager, you want to make sure that people have what they need to do a great job, develop and thrive. That might be a shared vision, a sense of engagement, or the new skills they need to create better results. Rather than, 'How do I make sure everyone's doing the right thing?' your start point might be, 'What do they need to succeed?' It may not seem a huge difference, but over time

> Your beliefs affect your sense of priority, on an everyday basis

it shapes your approach. It's a little like altering the course of a ship by a few degrees: quickly you end up somewhere completely different. Figure 3.2 looks at the values and beliefs of a coaching manager and predicts the skills and behaviours that result.

As a manager, when you believe that much of the value you add is to develop the people around you, you more naturally use coaching skills. For example, in one-to-one meetings with individual team members, you'll tend to focus on *them* in relation to the situation, rather than just the situation. In team meetings, rather than direct the discussion, you'll facilitate it more, as you prefer to encourage team members to be constructively involved. To a coaching manager, people's ability to be engaged, and to think for themselves, is more important than displaying their own knowledge. Clearly, that is a challenge for how we think we are perceived or add value as a manager, so I'll cover the tricky topic of the ego in Chapter 4.

Manager tends to coach	
Beliefs I operate from:	• Relationships with my team are based on equality • My subordinates can create great solutions • My contribution includes growing and developing people
Skills that I develop:	• Focussed listening, open questions, facilitation • Supportive challenge, constructive feedback • Empathy, relating to different character types
My typical behaviours include:	• I seek first to understand • I challenge interpretations, barriers or false limits • I encourage others to think and act responsibly
I learn not to:	• Quickly offer solutions • Eagerly display how knowledgeable I am • Control the direction of conversations
Things I make important:	• Creating a context in which I can coach others • The learning and development of people • People's ability to think and act for themselves

Figure 3.2 Values, beliefs and behaviours of a coaching manager

Develop your own style

The purpose of offering these two models is not to show either as right or wrong but simply to highlight the impact of your mindset or worldview. Indeed, it's likely that you may blend the two styles in a way that works, and Chapter 8, 'Build a flexible style of influence', is designed to help you do just that. Just remember that a lack of ability to coach creates a false limit upon you. If you are unable to coach, you are

> If you are unable to coach, you are more likely to argue that it doesn't work

more likely to argue that it doesn't work. When you have the skill to manage in both a directive and non-directive way, you can adapt to situations and people to produce consistently good results. Develop real flexibility and you have a true choice.

Pause and reflect

What are you making important?

Use the following questions to assess your own beliefs and mindset:

Q For you, what are the main skills of an effective manager? What must they do well?

Q How equal do you feel to the individuals in your team? Or how parental do you feel towards them?

Q When people around you make mistakes, how do you typically react?

Q Under what conditions would you be comfortable with your team learning through mistakes?

Q Reflecting on the two models (directive and coaching manager), which values and beliefs do you recognise as being relevant to your own?

Q As a manager, how does the pressure of a situation affect your ability to stay relaxed and flexible?

Q What three things could you do more of, or less of, that would improve the effectiveness of your management style?

If you're comfortable, ask the opinion of someone you trust to offer additional ideas or insights.

 In a nutshell

What is the mindset of a coaching manager?

As you develop coaching skills and behaviours in the workplace, it's good to consider your underlying beliefs as a manager. This is because your routine behaviours and responses flow from what you think is important. For example, if you want to be perceived as an expert or one who 'rescues' situations, then behaviours such as talking less and asking more feel unnatural. As an expert or 'rescuer', you are more likely to develop a directive style of giving ideas, opinions and solutions.

When you are aware of the beliefs or values that drive your behaviour, you can adjust. This might be as simple as remembering that 'Their ability to think is more important than me giving them all the answers'. When you focus on the beliefs of a coaching manager, you are more likely to interrupt your impulse to be directive and adopt a coaching style instead.

CHAPTER 4

How does our ego limit our ability to coach?

Here we'll discuss one of the potential barriers to coaching other people, which is our mind's perception of ourselves, or our ego. For example, we'll look at the ego's need to retain a sense of control during a conversation, perhaps by solving someone's problem or knowing the answer. I'll also explain how this compulsion runs much deeper than a learnt management style. I'll offer questions and ideas to help you become more aware of your ego and the strength of influence it can have upon you in your work environment.

Ego: What is the link to coaching?

One of the common barriers to a manager or leader being able to coach is their ego's typical drivers of a need to control events or to manage people's perception of them. For example, in work conversations, generally, we like to:

- Know what we are talking about
- Avoid saying anything dumb, inappropriate or wildly incorrect
- Be appropriate with the information or views we offer
- Stay mostly in the 'known', for example be able to understand what's being said
- Avoid causing ourselves (or others) embarrassment.

This is why when managers first learn to coach, they often find less directive coaching behaviours feel unnatural or awkward, for example as they operate from old beliefs of what it means to be a manager*, or simply a need to control what other people do. When you notice how your current self-image in the workplace affects your thoughts and behaviour in conversations, you can relax those 'auto-responses' more often.

Relate to someone else's views, by relaxing your grip on yours

To coach effectively, the influence of your ego, for example as expressed in your opinions or values, must be reduced in a conversation. Much of the potential of coaching comes from helping someone to think and act for themselves (without you telling them what to think). So, to be a good coach, you must be able to stay in a more neutral posture more often. For example, imagine that you are coaching a teenager on the topic of taking drugs. Does giving them your fierce (adult) views on that help? Or does it work better to relate to what it's like for a teenager growing up and to use that as a starting point? This is an extreme example, but a key tool of your influence is the ability to 'stand in someone else's shoes', and if you're too attached to your viewpoint, you will find that flexibility a challenge. Also, the value you can add for the person you're with is reduced.

The Ego: Who do you 'think' you are?

We all have an ego; it's a function of your mind. Your ego arises from your mind's tendency to create a concept of who you are (and who you are not). This also gives you your sense of identity; if I say, 'who are you?' or ask you to describe yourself, you might tell me your name, and then say things like, 'I'm a manager, team

---

*To review this idea again, have a look back at the charts (Figures 3.1 and 3.2) in the previous chapter, 'What is the mindset of a coaching manager?'.

leader, schoolteacher, doctor, father, mother', and so on. Depending on the circumstances, sometimes we give our age, where we are from, our religion, and so on. These descriptions and labels are your 'story of you', which has been stored by your ego as it tried to make sense of being you in the world. This 'story of you' also builds your self-image, for example 'I'm sporty, I'm creative, detail-focused, disorganised', and so on. Other attributes you might adopt include 'I'm a hard worker, good person, great manager, novice manager', and so on. Your mind has built these perceptions over time and now, you accept them, often without question. For example, maybe you're not as 'disorganised' or 'novice' as you imagine?

Our ego compares, contrasts and judges

To build this self-image, we compare ourselves to others and the world around us. This is natural and a function of our basic need to understand and keep ourselves safe; our ego-mind compares, contrasts and judges. Gradually, over time, your ego creates how it feels to be you in relation to the people and the world around you. So, when you create your self-image of being a manager or office worker, you automatically know what you are not, for example 'I'm not a doctor'. In doing this, the ego also maintains our sense of separation (as we notice what's different from us). This sense of separation, or difference, is natural; however, it can reduce our ability to coach, where our ability to build rapport and influence requires feelings of 'sameness'. I'll discuss the importance of both rapport and the relevance of sameness in Chapter 5, 'How to build rapport and relationship'.

In everyday life, our ego is a faculty of our mind and behaves almost like a background program, to influence our thoughts, decisions and feelings. For example, if you have a view that you're not a great people manager, you might use certain behaviours to cover that up or simply feel discomfort about that. Alternatively, you may imagine you're a fantastic manager and feel great about that. And, of course, both of those views are simply your perception, based on your observations, thoughts and comparisons.

 'Don't believe everything you think.'

Byron Katie

Our ego is both helpful and flawed

Some of the aspects of the ego are more helpful than others. For example, you might have a positive belief in yourself as a 'good' person, which gives you standards against which to judge your own behaviour. Perhaps you stop yourself from saying or doing

> Our ego can inform and misinform us

something unkind, simply because it didn't feel like 'you' to do that. However, it's less helpful when our egoic perception of 'I'm a good person' develops further into righteousness ('I know better than you') and places us in a position of being beyond fault ('Don't question me, I'm never wrong').

So, our ego can inform and misinform us. As our mind works to explain our experience of apparent separateness, it builds perceptions and beliefs we forget to question. Some of our concepts about ourselves are simply that – ideas and notions we created.

 'Your ego is a false identity that your mind constructed and then you took up residence in.'

Brandon Bays

How to measure the ego – size or strength?

Unfortunately, in common use, the term 'ego' is often used to describe an attribute of someone who appears arrogant or over-confident. We're familiar with the complaint, 'He/she has a

HUGE ego!' The truth is that we all have an ego, and it's neither 'big' nor 'small' – it's just our ego. If we wanted to assess our ego, it's more useful to consider its strength rather than its size, that is how much influence does your ego have upon you?

Our ego influences each of us in different ways and some of those ways are the opposite of the arrogance or overconfidence we often use to define the ego. For example, a person who explains that they are 'painfully shy' and finds it difficult to speak and express themselves in certain circumstances is also describing a strong egoic influence which acts upon them. They might also describe themselves as 'too self-conscious' or literally, too conscious of 'self'. When a shy person learns to relax this tendency, for example by focusing less on themselves and more on other people, they are often able to calm or reduce their feelings of shyness. The same trick can work for people who feel less comfortable making presentations or speaking to groups. When we focus on our audience and connect with them, we naturally relax our focus on our 'self', and so our sense of separation from others. We literally forget to feel self-conscious.

 Pause and reflect

How strong is your ego?

Use the following questions to become more aware of your ego; try to stay light-hearted with this. Working with this topic is more effective when we enjoy it.

Q How conscious are you of status or position – either your own or someone else's?

Q How good are you at being 'wrong'? For example, can you admit you are wrong? Can you apologise?

Q How much are you concerned by what other people think about you? Are you affected by their opinion or approval? ▶

(Q) What effect does criticism have upon you?

(Q) How much do you resist being controlled by other people in situations?

(Q) How much do you want to keep things the same and avoid change?

(Q) How easily embarrassed are you? How easily do you laugh at yourself?

Once again, perhaps ask someone whom you trust to offer additional views on your typical behaviour and tendencies.

Challenge your assumptions

The natural mistake we make is to assume that the ego *is* who we are, rather than viewing it as a constructed idea of ourselves or a list of ways to imagine that we 'should' behave. When we relax the grip of the ego, we reveal an increased feeling of connection to the world around us and a greater affinity to people, through a reduced sense of separation. This is just one of the reasons that for thousands of years, spiritual seekers have worked to free themselves from the influence (or 'fixations') of the ego. Seekers might go to extreme lengths, for example relinquish trappings of their former life, live more simply, maybe in isolation, even give up their former name, all with the intention to discover 'who they really are'.

Of course, you don't need to give up your life or even your day job to relax your ego. Instead, you might choose a simpler goal of 'everyday illumination' or awareness. This goal demands that you increase your awareness of the features and drives of your ego, to create more self-awareness and choice every day.

If you are interested to study this topic in more depth, I recommend *A New Earth* by Eckhart Tolle (Penguin, 2009). In his book, Tolle provides a clearer sense of our ego and encourages us to work with that in practical, everyday situations.

When imagined boundaries become false barriers to success

As we saw earlier, your sense of who you are includes your job role or title, for example, 'I'm a junior manager/senior manager'. It's all false, as all those roles are invented, along with the boundaries they suggest. In the workplace, we act as though the roles are real and that's logical as it helps to organise people's activities towards desired outcomes. Defined roles also help people to play to their strengths, for example, 'I'm a technical expert – that's what I'm good at and that's what people expect'.

However, sometimes it's helpful to challenge the assumptions that our imagined roles suggest. For example, if the organisation has defined you as a junior manager, does that make you apprehensive about speaking to groups of senior managers? And perhaps more comfortable speaking to groups of lower-ranked staff? Or, if you're a senior manager, how does it affect your behaviour in a meeting with people you have been told are more junior?

Three devices of the ego: Inflation, deflation and rigidity

Another way to spot the ego in action is to first appreciate its typical devices or methods. For example, the ego often uses the following three strategies:

1 *Inflation* – Here we build ourselves up, exaggerate or try to appear 'larger' or better in some way. For example, we might boast, or amplify our success, perhaps displaying 'showy' or ostentatious behaviour. The previous 'arrogant' behaviour we normally describe as a 'large ego' is an aspect of inflation. Please remember that whilst inflation is easily spotted when it's grandiose, inflation can also be subtle, for example dropping hints – 'Yes okay this cost is fine, you should see what I spend on restaurants in a month.'

2 *Deflation* – This is the opposite of the above; here we reduce ourselves, become shy, withdraw, 'play small', and

so on. We might underplay our own wants or needs, for example 'I'm not important.' This tendency has us feel 'lesser' in situations, or perhaps that we are an imposter in a senior role, for example 'the other board members know more than me.'

3 *Rigidity* – Here we are inflexible, intransigent or stubborn; we refuse to change or adapt, and so on. We might refuse invitations, advice or ideas because they trigger our innate resistance to change. This resistance can be overt and covert, for example 'I'll say no to doing something for you', or I'll just ignore your request.

Control helps us stay comfortable and safe

In the workplace especially, we have a natural compulsion to maintain our sense of comfort or surety by being in control. The nature of that control includes mental, emotional or actual/direct control, for example:

● Mental: To ensure we know what's happening/going to happen in a situation.

● Emotional: To suppress our feeling/emotions in a situation, perhaps we are upset but avoid displaying that, for example keep smiling.

● Direct: We use the force of our personality, will or position to direct events (make things happen).

Additional ways to illustrate egoic drivers for control include:

● Surety, for example 'I can trust this situation/person'

● The 'known' for example 'this all seems familiar'

● Sameness, routine, for example 'there's no surprises here'.

Conversely, the ego typically avoids the potential threats of:

● Unplanned/unexpected change

- Personal exposure, for example failure, embarrassment, being 'wrong'
- The unknown, 'I don't know anyone here/I have no prior knowledge on this subject', and so on.

In the workplace, think about how people might resist change or find it difficult to adopt new systems or structures – especially when they are unclear or confused about what the change means to them. This is one of the ways that coaching conversations can help people assimilate or handle change. Because when we help people express themselves, what they think and feel becomes clearer, which helps them to relax and decide what's important, for example for them and their work.

Your expression of, and need for, control is individual to you

For some of us, our need for control is obvious and we express that readily; for others, our need for control surfaces in subtle, even illogical, ways. For example, your colleague has been asked to draft and circulate a report on the environmental policy of the company and obtain initial feedback. By coincidence, this is a topic you already feel strongly about. You think that with even minor policy changes the company could make a big difference in its environmental impact, and you don't feel anyone is listening to your ideas. As you read someone else's thoughts on the subject, you feel annoyed and frustrated. In your view, the report doesn't go far enough and lacks clarity and impact. Your compulsion to control may range from trying to directly influence the report's content/messages, to changing the layout and headings and so on. Or, less logically, you might withdraw from commenting on the report, because the idea that you're not directly involved annoys you. This annoyance causes resistance (rigidity), and you isolate yourself further from the subject by not getting involved and disconnecting from the author of the report. In this case, the ego's drivers have effectively sabotaged your actions.

Use the questions below to consider your needs for, and expressions of, control.

 Pause and reflect

How do you seek to control?

This compulsion to control your world might be less obvious than the examples above, and the following questions can help you spot that, for example raise your self-awareness.

- **Q** How opinionated are you? For example, how strong are your opinions about certain things?
- **Q** How much advice do you give to other people?
- **Q** How do you behave (or feel) if you don't get your own way?
- **Q** How much do you control yourself in situations, for example 'I don't allow myself to do that' or, 'I would never do that'
- **Q** How well do you respond to unexpected change? for example your big meeting got cancelled, your taxi is really late, your friend just stood you up, or your house sale just fell through (again).
- **Q** When you feel controlled by other people and situations, how do you respond? For example, if you feel someone is dominating you – how do you feel/act?
- **Q** If you give someone good advice and they reject or ignore it, how do you feel?

Once again, perhaps ask someone whom you trust to offer additional views on your typical behaviour and tendencies.

The ego seeks the approval of others

One of the more well-known drivers of the ego is the approval of others, for example, when we judge that someone has a 'huge ego'. If we look more closely, we might notice a subtle indication that this person wants people to think well of them, for example to be impressive or maintain our respect. Other ways we might recognise this tendency in ourselves or others include:

- Wanting to be viewed in a certain way by others, for example as popular, attractive, kind, successful, special and so on.
- Wanting positions of status or respect, for example 'if I'm more senior I'll be more respected'
- Being upset if we imagine that others think badly of us or disapprove of us in some way.

This is all a natural part of being human by the way, and it's not bad (or good) to want to be viewed as popular or kind and so on. What's useful is to have some choice about that, for example 'I'd like to make the decision that would make me popular with my team right now, but it wouldn't be the right thing to do longer term'.

What's more important, control or approval?

In some situations, we want both control and approval. For example, things didn't go well in a recent work meeting, and you're bothered about that. Perhaps you got frustrated and said something harsh/negative, or maybe you lost your temper and upset the tone of the discussion. Thinking about the meeting troubles you, and you're not sure why; after all, you know that you were right in your opinions. In situations like this, we are upset because we have lost control, approval or both.

Using the example of the meeting, when you ask yourself, 'what was I seeking (that I lost), control or approval?' you may realise that:

- You feel you lost some approval, for example because other people in the meeting may have thought that your overreaction was unprofessional.

- The control you want is over your own temper.
- On balance, the potential loss of approval/respect from the group bothers you the most.

Use the exercise below to try this idea for yourself.

🏃 Ideas to action

Do you most want control or approval?

For a real situation, use the steps below to explore the features of your ego.

1   Identify/remember a situation that you are frustrated, concerned or uncomfortable about in some way. If you're really annoyed or upset, even better!

2   Consider the following question:

Q In this situation, what do you want most – approval or control?

If you can't decide, pause, sit with it and consider the idea. I am suggesting that your frustration/discomfort is caused by your ego because one of its needs (approval of others, or control) is not being met. Take your time, and try the idea on; what's most important to you about this situation, and how does that relate to the approval of others or control?

To move to a more resourceful view of the situation, consider the following questions:

1   What would it take for you to give up your need for approval/control (or both) in this situation?

2   If you gave up the need (for control or approval), what becomes possible – for example a fresh perspective, or a different response in the situation?

3   What are you deciding to do?

Rigidity, and the irrelevance of right and wrong

As earlier, the ego builds rigidity, for example, an attachment to how things should be, fixed views of what's right and what's wrong, or the avoidance of change. Where your ego is a strong influence on you, you often feel compelled to operate from this rigidity without question, for example 'I'm a manager, I should direct the activities of my team'. However, if you are to be an effective coach, your ability to remain objective or neutral in a conversation will help you get better results.

Imagine you're coaching someone and they criticise a colleague whom you know and trust. For example, maybe they've said that Mia is a liar and a fraud, and you don't agree with that (at all). Remember as a coach you are often a neutral facilitator of the process of the conversation. So, if you automatically leap to Mia's defence, that alters the nature of the conversation.

> Coach the person, not the issue

For coaching principles to work, we stay focused on the other person, explore their views, reflect those back and challenge them only if it's helpful to the conversation. Another way to say this is that you must coach the person, not the issue. So, your options are:

1 *Disagree with their view and contradict their opinion.* This is likely to create a sense of disagreement and reduce rapport as they are made to defend or justify their view. It may also distract the conversation onto a topic that's less relevant to the conversation, for example Mia and your feelings about what the other person has said.

2 *Ignore your disagreement and act as if you agree.* Possibly a worse option than the first, as you've traded your integrity for an attempt to please them, or at least avoid breaking rapport with them. You might say 'Yes, I can see, that's bad,

isn't it?' or 'Yes, I guess I can imagine her doing that'. If neither of those statements is true (because you can't see what they're saying or imagine Mia doing that), then that constitutes a lie and so your integrity is corrupted.

3 *Stay in a neutral posture and don't react to the critical nature of the remark.* This is generally the most effective option, as it retains rapport and so influence (plus integrity). Also, as you ignore your own desire to defend Mia, you retain an objective, impartial view of their remarks. For example, you can see beyond what that person is saying and stay interested in why they might say that. But by offering them neutral territory in which to consider their views, you help them to relax and become a little more objective. By listening and questioning further, you might loosen or relax that person's views. Perhaps as you ask them about their accusations, they explain themselves and perhaps realise that their view is a bit extreme.

Our goal is to develop flexibility – challenge

As a manager who coaches, sometimes you need to say what you think, and what you believe, or challenge what is being said. In Chapter 8, 'A flexible style of influence', I'll offer you the Steppingstones Model, in order to do just that in conversation, for example stay neutral or push back (both gently and firmly).

So, I'm not proposing that to coach you must ignore your own views, judgements and values. However, I do suggest that as you stay detached from your opinions, you can stay with the purpose of the conversation, which is to help someone think for themselves. Remember, a coaching conversation aims to create useful enquiry into a situation, to understand useful 'truths'

Coaching conversation aims to create useful enquiry into a situation

or 'knowns' about that. That enquiry requires a clear focus on the person being coached. As you relax the influence of your own ego in a conversation, you can create that clearer focus.

At a glance

Learn to quiet your mind

When we first discover the impact that our ego is having upon us, ironically, we may want to resist it, for example because we believe our ego is a negative influence upon us. Unfortunately, this type of resistance creates more stress or distraction because, in a fight with the mind, the mind keeps fighting. For example, when you notice your ego's impulses arise, (such as inflation, deflation or rigidity), you get annoyed with yourself. You literally start to 'think about thinking' and may get lost in that process.

During a coaching conversation, the best way to reduce the influence of your ego is to:

1 Notice it, acknowledge it (stay neutral): 'Oh, I'm trying to control their ideas here'.

2 Take a moment to quiet your mind, take a breath, and be still and calm for a moment (detach).

3 When your mind is quiet again, you are present and conscious, and you can choose what your best response will be, for example 'I'll ask them what they think'.

This is why the practice of 'mindfulness' or 'present moment awareness' is such a healthy one because when we are present, the mind is still/quiet – and so is the ego. Meditation is also hugely helpful because when we meditate regularly, we build our ability to quiet our mind more easily.

'The ego's greatest enemy of all is the present moment.'

Eckhart Tolle

This is personal and professional development

When we learn to reduce the influence of our ego upon us, we also develop greater emotional intelligence. Another way to describe this is that you have relaxed some of your rigid thinking and the conditioned responses that are based on egoic drives (inflation, deflation and rigidity). This enables any manager to use the principles of coaching more effectively. For example, as you coach someone else and they begin to criticise a decision that you (as their manager) have made, you are not automatically compelled to defend or justify that decision or take control of the conversation. Instead, you can remain in a neutral posture and stay interested to understand what your colleague thinks. It's less important whether the decision is a good one or not. It's more important that your colleague is uncomfortable with it and you need to understand that, and help them deal with it – or even change your view?

What are the benefits of a relaxed ego?

As a coaching manager (or in life generally), the benefits of learning to relax the influence of your ego in conversation include:

- less stress, for example from trying to keep control of situations, or resisting what you perceive as 'being controlled' by others
- increased sense of flexibility and 'easygoingness', for example by your decreased sense of attachment to how things are, or how they should be
- increased sense of 'possibility', for example working to maintain control takes effort and creates a false limit on what happens (or what you allow to happen)

- increased openness, trust, and relatedness to others as you become more 'real' to them (rather than the image of yourself that you work to project)
- increased sense of being 'freed up', as you don't always have to respond in predictable ways.

Of course, the above benefits also apply to the people that you coach (your coachees), although these are not things you can make happen directly. However, one of the natural outcomes of this style of conversation is that you may notice some of the above happens naturally. For example, as people feel listened to (and respected), they often relax their ego's rigidity or resistance to change.

How do I know my ego is *less* strong?

Of course, it's possible that you are very emotionally mature and that your ego has a much lesser influence on you than most people. See how many of the following apply to you.

- You're able to take direct criticism well, for example, you're relaxed about being proved wrong in a situation.
- You're not easily embarrassed, or you can laugh at yourself easily.
- You cope with unexpected change well, for example, you stay resourceful in a crisis.
- You can accept how things are, even when they're not how you want them to be.
- You're relaxed about issues of status or position.
- You're able to accept people with very different views from your own.
- You feel little need to impress, control or please people in situations; you don't get hung up on what other people think about you.

If your ego *is* less strong, it's likely that all these positive tendencies are more or less true for you, depending on the situation and personalities involved. Perhaps return to this list from time to time and see how your responses change.

In a nutshell

How does our ego limit our ability to coach?

Our ego, our sense of identity, is a function of our mind and can directly impair our ability to coach people. That's because our ego becomes a bundle of beliefs, stories about ourselves, behavioural drivers and conditioned responses. These drivers and predictable responses may contradict some of the core principles of coaching, such as equality, openness or a need to relate to someone else in their world.

As a manager who can coach a conversation, we recognise and reduce the influence of our ego upon us, for example to inflate, to deflate, to resist change and so on. We can then develop responses that are unaffected by the drivers or 'rules' of the ego. This enables us to stay flexible around the people we are coaching and be more present to their views and feelings.

PART 2

Ability

This part of the book looks at the basic skills of coaching for managers and offers ideas for how you might develop those further. We will focus on just the core skills, as these will help you the most as you coach in your workplace. The core skills of management coaching are:

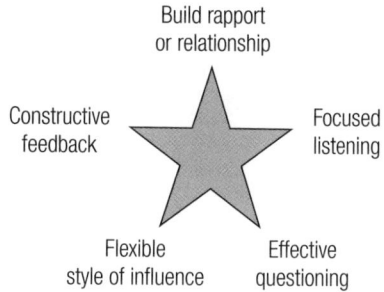

Build rapport
or relationship

Constructive
feedback

Focused
listening

Flexible
style of influence

Effective
questioning

There are obviously other skills that are useful, such as mindfulness, and the ability to observe non-verbal communication, but it's best to begin with the basics and lay a firm foundation on which you can build. Please remember that you already have some ability in all five skills – maybe you're already an effective listener, or maybe you promote warmth and trust easily. My aim is to help you develop in these areas further, for example by understanding why sometimes you don't listen as well as you might.

CHAPTER 5

How to build rapport and relationship

This chapter explains what rapport is and why it's relevant to your coaching. We'll look at the causes and features of rapport, so you'll know what affects it. You'll also be encouraged to think about how *you* experience rapport and how you might develop this important skill further.

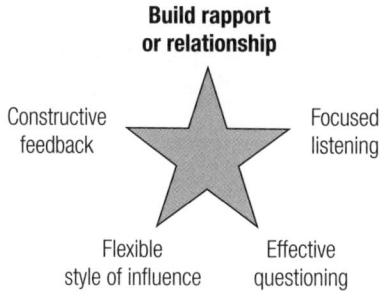

What is rapport?

Rapport is the sense of warmth and affinity in a relationship, either in a brief moment, like a quick conversation, or over time in a longer-term relationship. Rapport also refers to your quality of relatedness to someone else. That might be relatedness in the present moment, for example 'I'm feeling comfortable with this person', or it might refer to a relationship over time, for example 'I always enjoy talking to him/her'.

You may experience good rapport as feelings of warmth, comfort or 'sameness'. The rapport you feel with another person will affect your feelings and behaviour. For example, when you have good rapport, you are likely to feel comfortable and able to be yourself and act naturally. The other person is also likely to experience similar feelings as they, too, experience this sense of comfort.

> Two people with good rapport are also more likely to trust each other

Two people with good rapport are also more likely to trust each other, and their willingness to be open with each other will increase.

You might experience poor rapport as 'coolness' or a sense of being different from another person. This feeling of being 'different' from someone else might also create feelings of separateness or detachment. That may or may not be an issue, depending on your objectives in the situation. For example, it's helpful if you want to discourage a stranger from talking to you further.

A scale of rapport

There is a common misunderstanding that we either have or don't have rapport with someone. But where we are relating in any way to another person – for example in conversation, via email, on the telephone – then we are connecting to them. This connection creates a relationship of some sort, which is rapport. Whether that relationship is warm or cool is simply an indicator of the quality of that rapport. It's as if there are levels of rapport on a scale that moves above and below a neutral position. Figure 5.1 illustrates this idea of levels of rapport.

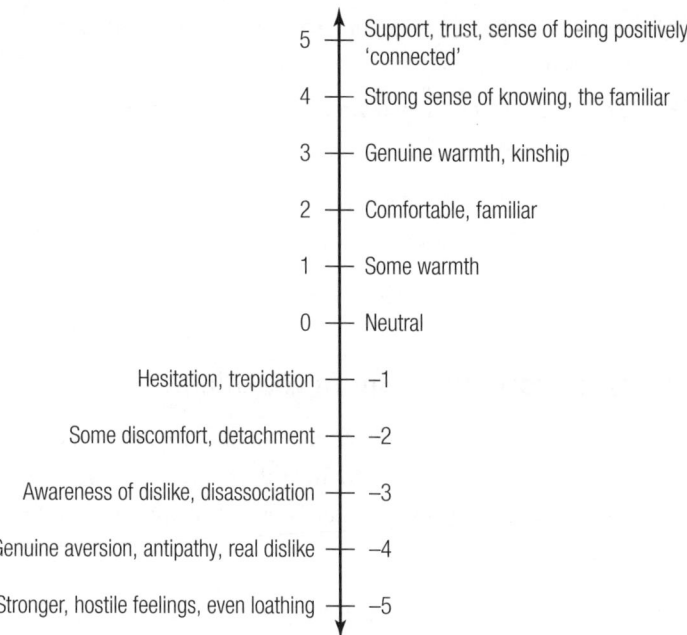

Figure 5.1 Scale of rapport

🐒 Ideas to action

Watch rapport in action

Choose a situation in which groups of people are present. Watch and listen for a while, then ask yourself the following questions.

Q How do you know if people are 'getting along well'? Look for physical, vocal and energetic matching, for example, are they as animated as each other?

Q What are the signs that people are cool or detached towards each other? Look for signs of mismatching.

Q In a conversation or in a meeting, what impact does good rapport have? ▶

Q How does 'detachment' or lack of rapport impact the quality of a conversation?

Q How does the quality of rapport in your work relationships affect collaboration and results?

As you notice the signs and impact of rapport, you naturally deepen your awareness and understanding of this topic.

Why is rapport important in coaching?

When we have positive rapport with someone, we create a climate of openness and trust between them and us. The comfort we then feel, helps people express themselves naturally. In coaching, positive rapport helps you to:

● influence someone constructively, that is without dictating to or 'commanding' them

● encourage people to think for themselves, as they are more comfortable pausing, reflecting and so on.

● challenge people or give them feedback in a way that builds confidence rather than discomfort

● be viewed as a supportive colleague rather than a critical threat

● have people trust you, and so be more open with you.

 Pause and reflect

Warm or cool – what's the difference?

Use the following questions to work with rapport principles for yourself.

1   Think of someone in a work situation with whom you feel you have *good* rapport, then ask yourself:

Q How do you feel when you're with them?

Q How do your feelings of good rapport with this person affect how you behave when you're with them?

Q How does this person seem the same as, or similar to, you?

2   Now think of someone in a work situation with whom you *don't* have good rapport. Try to choose someone with whom you want better rapport (rather than someone you simply don't like). Now reflect upon the following questions:

Q How do you feel when you're with this person, for example talking to them?

Q How do your feelings of poor rapport affect how you behave when you're with them? For example, how natural are you?

Q How does this person seem different from, or not the same as, you?

3   Finally, with the person with whom you don't have good rapport, consider:

Q What would the benefits be of having better rapport with this person? For example, how would things be different?

Q How do your thoughts or feelings of 'difference' affect you around this person?

Q How can you encourage feelings of sameness or relatedness? For example, asking 'What do we have in common here?'

What affects rapport?

Rapport is built on features of sameness. Basically, when we feel we are the same as someone else, we feel more connected to them than if we think we are different. These features of sameness can include:

- how we appear to someone, for example, physical appearance, clothing, racial background
- how we speak, for example, qualities of voice, energy, volume, speed
- what words we use, for example, the same jargon, key phrases

- the sameness or difference of our 'body language', for example, you use lots of hand gestures and so do I
- the values or beliefs we seem to have, for example, you're a vegetarian and so am I, or you support a certain football team, and so do I.

The above list is as relevant for boardrooms in business as it is for gang culture on the streets. Basically, when you look like me, sound like me, and seem like me, then I'll feel more comfortable with you. Try going to work in your gardening clothes and see the difference in how people respond to you (unless you work in a garden centre, of course). And if someone's accent or manner is very different from yours, does it take you a little longer to establish rapport? In the workplace or on the streets, we all have our buzzwords, common language or acronyms that distinguish us.

How to build rapport

When you have positive rapport with someone, you'll probably know. For example, you'll feel generally comfortable, and notice that they appear comfortable too. Where rapport is not an issue, then I'd suggest you reduce your focus on it and even forget about it. Understanding what impacts rapport is most valuable when you notice you haven't got it. As you feel less comfortable in a situation and are aware that there's an issue with rapport, then you can attend to that.

For most relationships in the workplace, you need to be in the positive ranges on our scale of rapport (Figure 5.1). Here are some indications of rapport dipping into the negative ranges.

- You have a sense of separation, detachment or difference.
- You're feeling less comfortable in the conversation, that is you're not being natural.

- You seem less able to express yourself or your ideas in a way that is understood.

- The other person seems lacking in warmth or openness towards you.

- The quality of mutual understanding is below what it needs to be.

In a situation where you want to build better rapport, the following exercise will help.

Ideas to action

Build better rapport

During a conversation where you notice that you don't have good rapport, try the following three-step process.

1   Relax! (breathe), come back to your 'centre' (a calm and relaxed state). This has many benefits, for example when you are calm and relaxed you can notice subtle signals. If you're stressed or frustrated it's more difficult to be aware.

2   Notice what might be causing a lack of rapport – look for major differences. Consider mismatches such as energy, body language or voice quality.

3   Have the intention to be more 'related' to the other person. For example, focus on a thought like 'I want to connect here, so . . . how are we the same?'

If you're relaxed, you've looked for what's causing a lack of rapport and have the intention to be related to the other person, you're very likely to notice something useful. For example, maybe you notice you've been doing most of the talking, or maybe the other person speaks with more, or less, energy than you do. Maybe the difference is what you both think about the situation (there's a lack of mutual understanding). You might choose to pull the conversation back to the starting point, for example, 'Okay, let's confirm ▶

what we're both saying here. Can you explain your view again?' When a person feels that you are genuinely listening to them, they are more likely to listen to you and your views. When mutual understanding is achieved, you can build on that.

By focusing less on differences, and more on how you are alike, you build rapport more easily. Your 'being alike' may encompass many different things, from gestures to values or a sense of what's important. However, your intention often makes the biggest difference. So have the intention to gain rapport, hold the thought for a while, and then let it go.

Empathy creates relatedness, which creates connection

Empathy is the ability to relate to another person on their terms and will help you to build rapport. Empathy requires that we notice another person's experience and sometimes how they're feeling. It can be as simple as saying 'I guess that's pretty frustrating for you'. When we notice and acknowledge someone, we create feelings of relatedness. For example, you might complain that your current workload means that you are working long hours. If I hear that and don't acknowledge that in some way, you may decide that I don't relate to your situation appropriately, or don't care. It may just take a simple remark like 'Okay, long hours, that's not great, is it? Let's look at what's causing that.' But if I'd simply said, 'Let's look at what's causing that', I might seem more detached from your situation.

Unconscious bias: The link to rapport

Unconscious bias refers to learned attitudes, beliefs or stereotypes that affect how we think and act daily. Our upbringing, education, country and location of origin, faith, religion and so on. can all create some level of challenge with unconscious bias. The list below highlights a few common examples:

1 Gender bias, for example that boys are better at maths and girls have better verbal skills.

2 Conformity bias, for example that adults educated at a prestigious academy or school will be smarter than someone who left school early to begin work.

3 Ageism., for example when someone is introduced to you as a new recruit into a low-level, administrative role and they appear to be close to retirement age, you assume that they are not ambitious or keen to learn new things.

4 Authority bias, for example if a senior person in the organisation says something, it's likely to be true, or a good idea.

5 Name bias, we prefer, or are more comfortable with, people when they have names that are culturally similar to our own, for example Anglo-Saxon, Asian, and so on.

Where higher levels of rapport, openness and trust rely on features of sameness, unconscious bias plays a role. For example, if you are introduced to someone from a region of the world where you have learned a harsh stereotype of their culture, you might begin the interaction with a negative sense of 'difference'. As a contrasting example, imagine that you are introduced to someone who reminds you of a much-loved friend or family member. In this case, your bias may well have you be unsuitably open, familiar or trusting in the situation. When you are unaware of your unconscious bias, or how it influences the levels of rapport with someone else, you are unable to challenge your thoughts and behaviour.

As the unconscious becomes conscious, we have more choice

When we are more aware of our learned stereotypes, assumptions and unproven beliefs, we can challenge them. For example:

● In ourselves – by working to think differently, shifting our perspective or simply acknowledging our bias, for example 'I'm not the best person to comment here, I simply don't have relevant experience/awareness'.

● In others – by encouraging others to shift perspective, for example 'I'm wondering if we're using outdated thinking here' or 'It might help to consider this from a more neutral perspective'.

Whilst specific reading and learning on this topic helps, so too does developing the skills of coaching. To acquire the skills of an effective coach, we must embark on a journey of personal and professional development. We are challenged to focus less on our own thoughts and feelings, and more on the opinions of someone else. As we learn the techniques of effective enquiry (through better listening, questions and intention to understand) we also relax our preconceptions and instinctive reactions. After almost thirty years of working with this subject, I have found this to be true, and I trust that you can discover this for yourself as well.

At a glance

Prepare in advance: Fast rapport principles

Let's say you've got an important conversation coming up and you want to be sure you build rapport easily. Here are some simple things you can do:

- Make sure you're feeling calm; for example, it often helps to breathe slowly from your stomach.
- Make sure that your attention is focused on the present; for example, notice what's happening 'right now'.
- Turn your attention to the person you want to establish rapport with and notice key aspects of their style. For example, how much energy do they display? How quickly or loudly do they talk? What's their physical posture - closed, open, and so on.?
- Use your intention to help you build rapport. For example, think 'How can I stay related to you?' and let this thought help you 'tune into' the other person and their world.
- Trust your ability to notice what you need to notice and, as you do so, make any adjustments necessary. For example, quieten your voice, smile a little more, or slow down as you speak.

Try these ideas initially somewhere where the stakes are lower, for example with a person serving you in a shop, or in casual conversation. Notice the things that seem to make the most difference for you, such as the idea of 'tuning in' or matching energy.

Rapport and the challenge of remote working

Where online meetings via Zoom, Teams and so on are more frequent, so is the challenge to build and maintain rapport and a sense of connection with others. When we are not physically in the same room, our ability to sense what's going on with someone else is impaired. Visually we are distracted, for example by a two-dimensional image, the screen itself, and our own physical surroundings. Through the natural sense of dissociation that occurs, we lose many of the non-verbal cues or our body's intelligence of how someone else is communicating. Our focus tends to shift more towards ourselves, our thoughts, and what's happening in our physical situation. So, our focus on what's happening with the person/people on the screen reduces. This means our empathy and our ability to relate to them begin to lower and we may miss the need to check in or reengage others back into the conversation.

The situation demands that we emphasise or even exaggerate our intention to display warmth and appreciation towards others. The following ideas can help in online meetings:

● Upfront: Make time for socialising, for example 'How are things with you?' or 'How's the family?' Instead of then moving on quickly, demonstrate genuine interest with follow-up questions, for example 'So, having a teenager full-time in the house sounds like a potential challenge, are you managing to not fight over the Wi-Fi?'

- During the meeting: Check in verbally more often, for example 'how does that sound?' or 'is this useful?'
- At the end of the meeting: Avoid a quick 'Right thanks, bye . . . ' and instead acknowledge someone in a way that is suitably personal, for example 'Okay, great, so thanks for your time here, that's been a good conversation for me, enjoy having your daughter back home for a while and let me know if you need more time on that budgeting process'.

In a nutshell

Building rapport or relationship

If you want to encourage others to be open to and trusting of you in a conversation, you must be able to create healthy levels of rapport. Rapport is built on features of sameness, and poor rapport normally indicates feelings of detachment or difference. By increasing your ability to relate to others on their own terms, you improve your ability to develop good rapport and therefore influence.

CHAPTER 6

How to be a better listener

This chapter identifies what it takes to listen effectively to someone else and what sometimes gets in the way of that. We'll look at the features of good listening, and what we mean by focused listening. We'll also explore ways of practicing listening to increase our normal capacity to listen.

Build rapport
or relationship

Constructive
feedback

**Focused
listening**

Flexible
style of influence

Effective
questioning

In a conversation where you aim to coach someone, your need to listen goes beyond a simple need to hear information. When we do not listen well, our understanding of someone and their conversation reduces, as does our ability to react appropriately. Yet when the quality of our listening is good, we can actually help someone to speak and express themselves. It's as if they recognise they are really being listened to, and so can relax and simply speak; if

> Good listeners build rapport and warmth more naturally, through their increased focus on other people

you've ever been partially ignored as you tried to explain something, you already know this. Good listeners build rapport and warmth more naturally, through their increased focus on other people.

Listening begins with intention and concentration

The quality of your listening is directly linked to the quality of your attention. So good listening demands that you make a conscious effort to listen. Your intention to listen begins with that.

> Good listening demands that you make a conscious effort to listen

You also need a clear mind, free of chatter – and that flows more easily from your simple intention to listen. When we're 'kind of' listening to someone (and not really), our attention is partly on the person we are with, and partly on our own thoughts. I call this 'cosmetic listening', as it has a superficial or cosmetic quality to it. Occasionally this quality of listening may be okay, for example when listening to the chatter of a small child. However, it is ineffective within a coaching conversation. If you are going to be a good listener, poor concentration, being distracted and generally not making the other person important are all barriers that you must overcome. Developing a strong intention, clear focus and concentration will help you with that.

Self-awareness check

How well do you listen?

Reflect on a recent conversation (or do this exercise after your next conversation). Then ask yourself:

Q How busy (or quiet) was your mind during the conversation?

Q While the other person was talking, how much of your focus (or attention) was on what **they** were saying and how much was it on what **you** were thinking?

> **Q** During the conversation, were you having any persistent thoughts or feelings? If you were, how did those thoughts affect your listening?
>
> **Q** If we asked the other person to describe how 'listened to' they felt during that conversation, what do you think they would say?
>
> **Q** What would it take for you to be a better listener?
>
> Use your responses to change your approach in future conversations. Try listening to someone in a different way and see if you can improve the quality of your listening.

Develop your power of attention

The basic principle of good listening is actually that you need to 'be with' the person you are supposed to be listening to. This requires that you develop a clear focus on them. What stops your attention from being on another person is a combination of internal and external distractions. Internal distractions include your thoughts, judgements or 'mind chatter'. External distractions range from your mobile phone, alert messages from your laptop, to your physical situation (room noise, etc.) – or simply anything you allow your attention to shift to.

As we coach, we increase our focus or attention on the person we are with. Imagine your attention as the beam of a torch you can adjust by twisting the lens. If you broaden the arc/span of the beam, then that dilutes the brightness of the light. When you reduce the arc of the torch beam back down, then the light gets brighter; so it is with listening. Try it now; how clear is your attention on this book? And what might be distracting your focus from other things? Notice the impact of your focus on the quality of your experience at this moment.

During a coaching session, you need to be able to maintain this proper attention for long periods of time. Depending on what type of coaching you do, some sessions can be lengthy, for example more than 30 minutes, and maintaining effective listening for that long isn't something most people can do.

Please stay positive about your ability to develop this proper attention. With regular practice, listening is a muscle that develops naturally over time. You simply build that from whatever your current ability is. For example, consider:

● When you are in work conversations, how scattered or focused is your attention?

● What distracts you from maintaining focused attention on someone else?

● In work conversations, what would you have to give up, or stop doing, to create better attention on other people?

A good way to increase your capacity to create stronger attention in this way is to practise 'present-moment awareness' – this means you must clear your mind and focus on what's happening right now. The following exercise will help you to do this.

Ideas to action

Practise present-moment awareness

This exercise can help you stay present both to yourself and to other people. If you know you tend to 'live in your mind', it's also a good way to ground yourself back into reality. As your mind naturally falls quiet from troubling thoughts, it's also a way to reduce stress. Use this anywhere (and everywhere) to practise being present.

● *Notice your surroundings.* Start to notice your immediate surroundings in more detail, by turning your attention to them. First, listen. What sounds can you hear? What can you see? Next, look at things afresh, notice some detail, and register where you are and what's happening (or not happening).

- *Notice your body.* Now notice your body in its current position and posture. Check how your body feels, perhaps move a little more, and get a stronger sense of being in your body. Then check your breathing. As you breathe, how is your stomach affected by that?

- *Quiet your mind.* Next, notice your mind and how much activity is happening, for example how much thought activity is there? As thoughts are not needed for this, simply refocus on being in your body, in the environment you're in right now. Clear your mind by focusing on what's happening in your physical environment. To reconnect with your body, try checking your breath, or moving your fingers or toes. As thoughts drift in, simply notice them and refocus on what's happening now.

Filtered listening – unconscious bias

Just as important as our effort to listen is our sense of purpose, which affects *how* we listen. For example, if I listen to you as if you are someone who doesn't know very much, then my assumption will cause me to filter what you say for things that confirm my belief. Alternatively, if I intend to listen to you as someone who has great knowledge, then the manner of my listening is changed. Imagine sitting down with someone like Barack Obama and asking him what he thinks about environmental issues. Then, imagine asking your next-door neighbour the same question – how would your listening be different?

Your beliefs about these two people may/may not affect how you listen to them. For example, pearls of wisdom spoken by your next-door neighbour may not have as profound an impact upon you as the same ideas spoken by a statesman. That's why subjective qualities such as charisma or positive reputation are so highly prized where influence is someone's key to success. They have a marked effect on someone's ability to convince or persuade, as they create positive filters for an audience's listening.

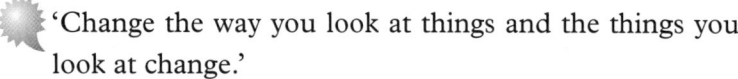 'Change the way you look at things and the things you look at change.'

Dr Wayne Dyer

Listen from nothing – reduce your unconscious bias

A specific posture I'd encourage you to develop is your ability to listen 'from nothing'. That is, as you listen to someone, have no assumptions about them or what they are saying. As you listen, experience them as they are in that moment, and focus on what they are saying – in that moment. It's a practical experience of being present to them. Your mind is free of judgement-type thoughts based on your previous experience of them, as though you now listen to them afresh. We have a sense of being with them, rather than being in our own mind with our thoughts. When you listen in this way, your mind is mostly still and quiet, as your focus is on what the other person says.

Listening 'from nothing' is a challenge, as we need to clear our minds of what we already think about a person, based on our experience of them. Even if we've only just met someone, we form quick opinions or judgements about who we think they are and what they are like. As in Chapter 4 on your ego, and how it affects your ability to coach, good listening demands that we reduce the importance of ourselves in a conversation, and instead focus on the person we are coaching. The following will help you to stay focused on someone else in a conversation, (rather than on your thoughts about them).

🏃 Ideas to action

Reduce your unconscious bias

Use the following process in advance of a conversation where you want to develop (and demonstrate) better listening.

Step 1. As you prepare to begin the conversation

- Stay calm and relaxed. Use steady breathing and an upright, open posture to help maintain a feeling of peaceful strength.

- Decide your positive intention for the conversation, for example 'I want to gather the key facts from this conversation', or 'I want the other person to feel heard'.

- Continue to stay calm and relaxed, stay present, listen to your surroundings, and attune to what is happening.

Step 2. During the conversation

- Maintain a calm and focused attention on the person you are listening to. Use your body to demonstrate (and enable) effective listening, for example, face someone directly, and maintain an open posture towards them.

- Maintain your attention (and demonstrate interest); ask questions such as 'Can you say more about that?' or make observations or summarise what has been said.

- Any time your attention wanders, confirm your intention, for example 'I want to stay focused on the key facts here'.

Step 3. After the conversation

- Reflect on what went well and what you want to improve. Note down your ideas; for example, 'Stay focused on what they're saying, rather than what I'm thinking'.

Barriers to listening – what stops us?

None of us intends to be a poor listener; unfortunately, the barriers to good listening are many and varied. Sometimes our attention is on ourselves and our thinking, rather than on the other person. Perhaps our minds may be buzzy with thoughts or ideas. Or perhaps we want to talk about things that are important to us. For example, as someone is talking to you about something they feel is important, you may be having related, but different, thoughts, such as 'All this talk about miscommunication is fine, but I just want to know the reason the team isn't talking to each other.'

Another natural, human tendency is to want to put something of ourselves into the conversation, perhaps to impress the other person or make them like us. For example, someone might begin to explain a current issue they have at work, and you relate to it totally. You might say 'Ah, yes I've had something similar happen to me, let me tell you about it . . . ' So, you distract them from completing their story and sharing their understanding of that. As a coach, you have turned the focus of attention off them and onto you and they may be distracted or frustrated by that. As it's the other person who is sharing their issue, and you haven't yet explored it properly, the potential benefit of your listening to them effectively is lost.

Talking about our own experiences doesn't make us bad people – we often don't intend to distract the conversation from the speaker. In some conversations, it's okay and quite fun to do so, for example, 'Oh, you think that's bad? – hey, I can beat that one!' It depends on the situation and our intentions for that. The issue is our poor self-awareness, where we don't realise that we hijacked a conversation and we have reduced the quality of that conversation as a result. In the previous work example, if I don't notice that I'm telling my story about a 'similar thing that happened to me', then I'm unlikely to stop myself from doing that.

But when I recognise that what I'm doing distracts from the importance of the other person explaining their current issue, I can ignore my own urge to interrupt.

In a nutshell

Focused listening

For any manager and coach, focused listening is a valuable skill to develop. When we listen properly to someone, we can literally increase their ability to express themselves. When we are a skilled listener, we tap into a rich seam of understanding and influence. What stops us from listening in any situation is simply ourselves. Either we are distracted by our own thoughts or ideas, or we simply don't make the effort to focus on someone else. Really good listening demands that we make the other person more important in the conversation and let go of the importance of ourselves. As we really focus on someone else with the intention of listening fully to them, the sense of ourselves, our ego, diminishes.

CHAPTER 7

How to ask effective questions

here coaching works by creating conversations of effective enquiry, then clearly the ability to ask great questions is a core skill. In this chapter, we will look at the principles of effective questioning, plus some simple dos and don'ts. I'll offer examples of questions you might use more often, plus some with a specific purpose, for example, to broaden a debate, shift someone's perspective or gather more specific information. You'll also find an exercise to help you start to ask better questions right away.

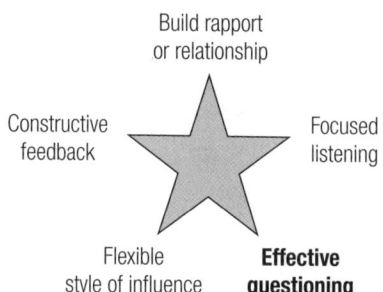

Great questions: A neat trick

People who ask quality questions generally obtain richer information and understanding. Have you ever sat in a meeting where someone asked a really great question about a situation? Perhaps the conversation had become disjointed or difficult to comprehend. Or maybe people seemed to have very different views and agreement seemed unlikely. Then someone asked a really good question. What effect did it have on the group? Good questions can have profound influence on a situation, perhaps by crystallising debate or addressing the heart of a matter. Or maybe they save time, as they bring things back on track. When you ask a great question, it can often be of greater value than offering an idea or an opinion. And yet in the workplace, we tend to put more of our effort into forming ideas or opinions, which we then explain from our perspective. Our views and ideas then compete with those of other people, as we work to stay ahead of the conversation.

In coaching, a well-timed, simply worded question can turn keys, unlock doors and provoke insight for the person you're coaching –

> A well-timed, simply worded question can turn keys, unlock doors and provoke insight

maybe a question such as 'If you could change just one thing about this situation, what would that be?' or 'What's important about this to you?' As the benefits of coaching rest upon our ability to have others think for themselves, the quality of our questions eases their progress.

What are the attributes of an effective question? In coaching, a good question:

- is simple
- has a clear sense of purpose
- influences someone's thoughts and understanding – without being controlling.

At a glance

Coach the person, not the issue

Remember that your focus during a coaching conversation is to help the person fix the issue - not for you to fix the issue. So, ask questions that help *them* think about the situation, rather than help *you* think about the situation!

The power of keeping things simple

Great questions are not complicated; they are simple in their construction. If someone must struggle to understand your question before they can attempt to answer it, you risk wasting energy and confusing someone. For example, try answering the following question:

Q Considering the current nature of our world and our organisations as forming part of that world, what are the key obstacles that seem to pose the greatest prevailing threats to the ability of organisations to contribute constructively to our environmental issues?

How did you like that? It takes me right back to school exam papers! The question is long, complicated and seems to be 'getting at something', that is that there is a 'right' or 'wrong' response. It's off-putting in its tone and extreme just to prove a point. Let's simplify it a little and see how that changes the impact it has upon us:

Q What are the key obstacles that pose the greatest threats to the ability of organisations to contribute constructively to our environmental issues?

It's better when we have stripped away the pointless words, but we must still work to comprehend the meaning before we can use mental energy in forming our response. Words such as *key obstacles* and *constructively* seem significant – even though their meaning is unclear. Again, the question feels a little highbrow or 'exclusive'. Let's try another level of simplification:

Q As organisations try to help with environmental issues, what barriers do they face?

This question feels different, doesn't it? Now, rather than trying to understand what the question is asking us to do, we can focus our energy on our response. This example encourages your answer, as it has no 'cleverness' built into it. It is less intimidating or pressured – as though anyone can have a valid opinion. Therefore, when we want to ask effective coaching questions, we simplify language and use shorter/simpler words and terms.

The following table offers further examples of simple and complicated questions.

Complicated question	Simpler version
What are the various issues or complications that have led us to where we are with this situation?	What's caused this?
Considering the after-effects of such an action, what are the consequences of such a move, do you think?	How will doing that affect things?
What kind of opinions or views might Tomasz bring to the table here, do you think?	What does Tomasz think about this?

And if those sound obvious, don't be fooled! Try listening to people in meetings or professional discussions and focus on the questions people use. Here are some reasons we use overly complex questions in the workplace:

- **We like to appear smart, clever and knowledgeable** So, we overcomplicate a thought or question, instead of using the simplest version. The simple question 'What does Tomasz think?' may save time, focus the debate, and provide a shift in perspective – but we don't sound 'professional', which may be a stronger urge.

- **We start talking before we have a clear version of our question** Our urge to talk, to be part of a conversation, may have us start a statement before we know where we are going with it. Clear questions demand clarity of mind and thought, which sometimes means we first need to maintain a relaxed, yet focused, state of mind.

- **We are uncomfortable asking what we really want to know** Instead of asking a direct question, we 'strategise' around it. For example, as someone explains what a problem is, we become confused. Maybe the problem appears to have changed during the explanation. But we don't want to look stupid, so we try to gain clarity without saying 'I'm confused'.

The dialogue below demonstrates a general use of ineffective questioning:

Naomi	'I'm fed up with the way Finance think that they can just change the way things are going to get done and then expect everyone else just to fall in line with whatever new piece of documentation they've invented. It's ridiculous.'
Manager	Why? What documentation changed?
Naomi	'No, they haven't changed anything, it's just that they've implied that they might do. Gemma in particular is really worried now.'
Manager	[thinks] *I'm a bit confused . . . what's the issue here?* [asks] 'Why is Gemma worried?'
Naomi	'Well, because she's the one who's going to have to cope with the new documentation.'
Manager	'I thought there wasn't any new documentation?'

Although the manager is confused, they are reluctant to admit that. So, they keep asking questions and hope they'll eventually get clarity. They might get clarity – or they might not. It's likely they'll waste time pursuing different lines of enquiry (like 'What documentation 'might' be changing?').

Here's how asking the question that first occurred to them affects things:

Naomi	'I'm fed up with the way Finance think that they can just change the way things are going to get done and then expect everyone else just to fall in line with whatever new piece of documentation they've invented. It's ridiculous.'
Manager	'Why? What documentation changed?'
Naomi	'No, they haven't changed anything, it's just that they've implied that they might do. Moira in particular is really worried now.'
Manager	[thinks] *I'm a bit confused . . . what's the issue here?* [asks] 'So, Naomi, I'm a bit confused, what's the issue here?'
Naomi	'Well, it's generally just their complete lack of consultation with us, they just don't ever keep us in the loop.'

Again, it's a simple example to prove a point. When we ask what's really on our minds, rather than rewording it or translating it into something slightly different, we retain the integrity of our first impulse. Our first impulse is often the clearest thought we have, and the one that can create the greatest clarity in a situation. It's often a simple thought – and so 'not very clever' and less appealing to us as a question we want to voice publicly.

🏃 Ideas to action

Go ask some questions . . .

Next time someone starts telling you about a problem (or starts complaining), try asking some (or all) of the following questions:

Q What else/who else is affected by this?
Q What's causing this, do you think?

(Q) What needs to happen then?

(Q) What options are you considering?

(Q) So, what have you decided to do?

As you can see, each question has a different purpose. Individually, each question may be productive, and together they create a sense of forward movement, that is towards solution and action.

When clever isn't clever . . .

Our tendency to value apparently 'intelligent' debate over simplicity stops us from asking great questions. So does our unwillingness to appear like the only person in the room who doesn't understand what is being said. Have you ever sat in a meeting feeling really confused about the discussion and stayed quiet? Then someone else declared their confusion, asked for clarification and it was useful to everyone? The conversation had become confused or irrelevant and yet most of the group had avoided asking for clarification. A neat question was all that was needed to pull things back on track. In coaching conversations especially, simple questions born from a clear intention create effective progress.

> Simple questions born from a clear intention create effective progress

🏃 Ideas to action

Learn from your surroundings

The following exercise will help you become more aware of the quality of questions you typically hear – and those that you yourself ask.

Pick a conversation where people are discussing something as a group. If you are part of that group, you can also consider your own contributions ▶

afterwards. Listen to the types of questions that are being asked and reflect on the following:

- How often are people asking questions, and how often are they simply responding to what has been said?
- What impact does a lack of questions have?
- When people do ask questions, how effective are they? for example what impact do their questions have on the quality of discussion?
- Which types of questions work well – and which don't?
- If you asked questions, what was your intention or purpose behind those questions?

Finally, when you have observed the tendencies of yourself and others, take some time to consider how you might improve the quality (and impact) of your own questions.

Questions with a clear sense of purpose

Another attribute of an effective question is that it has a clear purpose or objective. For example, that clear purpose may be to gather more information, to encourage ideas or to motivate someone to act. When we don't have a clear sense of purpose behind our question, the question will often be confusing or get a result that we didn't want. In coaching, this is important because you want your questions to help the conversation make progress in some way. The following table illustrates questions with a clear purpose. They are also nice, simple questions you might use in your everyday work situations.

Purpose	Coaching examples
Gather general information	Can you say more about that?
Gather specific information	Specifically, what is it that you're unhappy about?
	Can you tell me what actually happened?

Purpose	Coaching examples
Help someone remember something more clearly	What else can you remember?
To refocus someone on what's important, for example, keep them on track, or calm them down	Okay, so what's really important about all this? What seems to be the most important thing for us to focus on now?
Understand someone's values	What is important to you about that? Why is that important to you?
Help someone appreciate another person's perspective	What might be Bharat's reasons behind asking for this? What's important to Bharat? If Bharat was here, how would he describe this situation?
Get someone to link two thoughts, or situations, together	How do your work pressures relate to what you said about developing the team more?
Help someone come to a conclusion	What are your thoughts about this now? What is the conclusion you are drawing from this now?
Produce ideas without a sense of pressure	What options are there? What options are available to you? What things might you do? What ideas are you having now?
Influence someone to decide	Which option do you prefer? What have you decided to do?
Influence someone to action	What could you do about that right now?
Prepare someone to overcome the potential barriers to taking action	What might stop you from doing that? [Follow-up] So how will you overcome that?

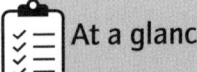

At a glance

Is this a closed question?

To coach effectively you'll want to develop an ability to ask consistently open questions, that is questions that cannot be answered with a 'yes' or a 'no'. These questions literally open up discussion and target a broader range of potential responses. To remind you, open questions begin with:

- what
- when
- where
- who
- why.

Consider the benefits of asking more open questions in your everyday conversations. *What* difference could that make? (And *how* could you start right now?)

Strategising or 'leading the witness'

Remember, in coaching, we encourage others to be more self-directed, so, our questions must also have an *open intention*. Questions with an open intention are unattached to any particular outcome or response. They include questions such as 'What do you think?' or 'What is possible?' Questions with a closed intention assume fewer potential options as a response, for example, 'In order to not upset her further, what would your conscience tell you to do?' This question dramatically closes down the options of an open response. Sometimes this type of question occurs when the manager wants to make the other person realise something they think is true, as in the previous example, 'I think you need to make amends here'.

When we ask a question and we know what we want someone's answer to be, it's a subtle form of direction or control. Please be willing to ask questions that you don't know the answer to.

> **Be willing to ask questions that you don't know the answer to**

When we first learn about the basic ideas of coaching, for example 'ask, don't tell', asking strategised questions is an easy trap to fall into. That's because we know we need to avoid being overly directive and let someone else come up with their own answers, but we still want to help or guide someone to get to a solution. And so, we ask questions with an underlying strategy instead.

The following table includes examples of strategised questions, alongside questions with a more open intention.

Strategising question	Question with a more open intention
Couldn't you speak to your boss about this?	What support do you need with this?
Have you considered putting a plan together to make everyone agree to the dates?	How can you get everyone to agree to the dates?
How angry are you about all this?	How are you feeling about this?
What could your HR representative do to help you?	Who else might help? [Or even more open] What are you thinking of doing?
Didn't you say that Maria doesn't actually want to be involved anyway?	How would Maria feel about that?

As you can see, the strategised questions seem to have more of an agenda – as though the person asking them is pointing at something or has an opinion about what the answer should be. We sometimes call this 'leading the witness', because the person asking the question appears to be using a subtle form of direction to reach a fixed conclusion. In coaching, these types of questions are less effective than open questions, because they reduce the openness, creativity and engagement of the person being coached.

At a glance

Check your tone of voice

A great question can be wrecked by lousy tonality. For example, try asking the question 'Why did you do that?' out loud in the following ways:

- as if you think the person is the stupidest you've met in a long time
- with a big smile in your voice and demeanour
- with a gentle, neutral tone

There's also a pitfall to using questions that begin with the word 'why', as they can cause people to be defensive or to feel they need to justify themselves. So, remember to be careful using 'why' and soften your tonality. Try to stay neutral with your demeanour, so that the person feels less judged by the question and so will feel less cautious with their response.

Powerful questions

In conversation, people sometimes get 'stuck' in a problem, for example, they only want to talk about the issue and not any potential solutions. So powerful questions are a very useful tool as they encompass a statement of the problem and propel it towards a solution. A powerful question can turn someone's energy away from describing or justifying an issue and towards more constructive thought. Also, by adopting a solution focus we help lighten the mood of a situation – away from frustration and towards optimism.

Attributes of powerful questions include:

- acknowledging the issue or challenge
- assuming that a positive outcome is possible
- they are open (what, how, etc.) and provoke a creative response.

In the workplace, we are often faced with complaints or issues that ignore the *possibility* of a solution, for example, 'We can't do this' or 'This is an impossible situation'. As a coach (or a manager), much of the value you add is to create a sense of possibility in a situation that helps people to move towards a solution. The following table illustrates this idea further.

Statement of issue/complaint	Powerful question
It's hopeless – we're never going to get it done by Friday because we've already got so much other work in the queue.	How can we get it done by Friday and still deal with the other work in the queue?
We'd love to have a staff summer party again, but the money needs to go on training this year.	How can we have a summer party *and* still afford the training?
We really need to do some team building to improve collaboration, but people's roles are going to change, and we don't yet know what that's going to mean.	How can we do some team building and still support the new roles in future?

In a nutshell

Effective questions

In coaching, effective questions provoke valuable thoughts and reflection and help surface insight, clarity or even a decision to act. Effective questions are simply worded so that someone puts their

▶

effort into forming their response, rather than on understanding the question. Effective questions also have a clear sense of purpose, for example, to gather more information, to switch perspectives, or create a sense of the future. When our questions are open, simple and have a clear purpose, people can respond to them freely and openly. So, when you coach, it's important that your questions have a mostly open intention, that is they are unattached to any fixed outcome.

CHAPTER 8

Develop a flexible style of influence: The Steppingstones Model

Our fourth skill is your ability to adopt a flexible style of influence during a conversation. We'll look at the ways you currently influence someone in a conversation and identify the different impacts of those. We'll build on previous coaching ideas, for example, directive and less directive styles, and show how you do not have to choose between the two. When you know the behaviours that sit between 'tell' and 'ask' you can move between or combine styles, and the Steppingstones Model will help you do this. As you'd expect, I'll offer hints, tips and guidance to encourage you to get the most from the ideas.

Build rapport or relationship

Constructive feedback

Focused listening

Flexible style of influence

Effective questioning

What do we mean by 'flexible style of influence'?

As a quick reminder, there are two basic 'ends' to our spectrum of influence as Figure 8.1 illustrates – 'tell' and 'ask.'

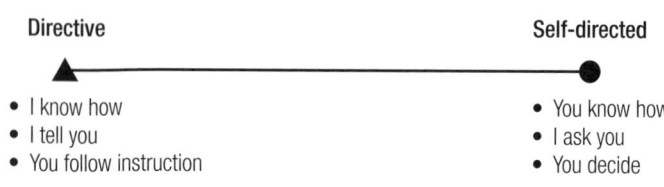

Figure 8.1 Spectrum of influence

Why is flexibility important to develop?

You'll remember that a coaching conversation influences the thoughts, behaviour and learning of another person. We do that

> A coaching conversation isn't just you asking lots of questions of someone else

by being less directive or 'tell' and instead we use effective listening, questioning, offer feedback, and so on. However, it's important to notice that a coaching conversation isn't just you asking lots of questions of someone else.

Consider that idea for a moment: imagine all you're allowed to do during a conversation is ask questions, nothing else. For you, as questioner, you might feel constrained or even frustrated. You might want to say things, and make observations, but feel like you're not allowed to do that. As a manager, you might also hear

> The conversation needs to feel natural for you and natural for the person you're with

things that don't make sense, or that you know you can't allow to happen. For the person being coached, a list of questions with no 'input' from you might feel odd, and unnatural, and potentially puts them under pressure.

The conversation needs to feel natural for you and natural for the person you're with. So, to stay effective and retain your sense of comfort during conversations, you need to use other behaviours. This helps you move from being more directive when that feels right, and then return to a less directive and encouraging style. For example, to give an opinion, and then return to a less directive style by asking a question.

At a glance

Convince yourself to coach

When you are first learning how to adopt a coaching style, I encourage you to use the less directive behaviours of silence, asking questions, giving summaries and making observations, more often than jumping in with advice or instruction. By truly learning how to 'sit back' in the conversation, and do less (literally work 'less hard'), you will experience the benefits of a less directive style for yourself. For the person you are coaching, they are likely to feel more listened to, respected and also positively challenged for example to share their own views and ideas.

The Steppingstones Model: Two ends of a scale, with behaviours in between . . .

Some language is clearly directive and attempts to influence directly, for example, 'I want you to do this'. Other language encourages someone to decide for themselves, for example, 'What do you want to do?' Between these two extremes are behaviours that exert different strengths of influence. For example, if I make an observation on or about something you have said, this will have a more neutral impact on you than if I gave you direct advice (see Figure 8.2 The Steppingstones Model).

Let's look at the different behaviours of The Steppingstones Model and reflect on how you might use them. We'll start with the less directive behaviours and move towards the more directive end of the scale (from right to left of the figure).

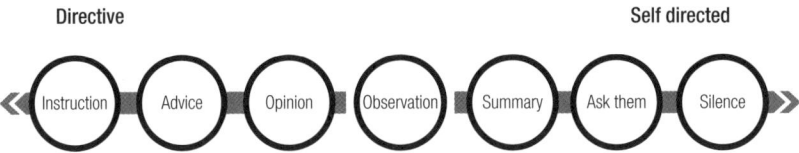

Directive   **Self directed**

Instruction   Advice   Opinion   Observation   Summary   Ask them   Silence

Figure 8.2 The Steppingstones Model

Self-awareness check

How much flexibility do you already have?

Use the questions below to increase your self-awareness in this area. Another way to do this would be to have someone observe how you typically influence others, for example in a meeting, and then ask them to answer the questions on your behalf.

Q During a work conversation, what seems more important: giving your opinion or making an effort to understand someone else's?

Q How often do you simply summarise what someone's said, without adding your own opinion or ideas immediately afterwards?

Q How often do you make observations about what someone is saying, simply to draw their attention to something that might help them, that is without following up with your own view?

Finally, spend time reflecting on how much you feel able to relax your need to influence at all in a conversation. For example, might it be possible for you to simply facilitate a conversation, with no input on the content or direction of that conversation?

Behaviour 1: Say nothing

The behaviour of 'saying nothing' is a little strange to imagine as an influencing style, yet silence as a response to what someone has just said can sometimes be perfect. Silence enables someone to pause, reflect on what they've just said, or perhaps go deeper into what they are saying. It suggests calmness from you and allows the other person to relax and speak with the sense of ease that you have created. It also helps you to really listen to the other person, perhaps observing their body language or energy.

Like all the behaviours described here, overusing silence can have the reverse effect and cause the other person to feel tense because you're not responding to them verbally. When silence becomes too uncomfortable for the person you're coaching, you'll notice by their non-verbal signals, for example, changes in their posture, tone or facial expressions. Some signals are clear indications that you need to speak, for example, if they stop speaking and look directly back at you with an expectant expression. Other signals are subtler, for example over time you may notice signs that they appear frustrated or tense.

Behaviour 2: Ask an open (neutrally worded) question

For a question to have the least directive style of influence, it should be both open and worded as neutrally as possible. For example, 'Do you think you should plan the meeting in advance with Benji?' is closed as it can be answered simply with a 'yes' or 'no'. The question also tries to direct because you're suggesting they should plan the meeting. A more neutral question might be 'How will you prepare for the meeting?' Although this question is still mildly directive, as you've suggested preparation is necessary, it may be both appropriate and helpful (to help someone think the preparation through). Alternatively, you might be guiding the person too specifically/strongly, perhaps because they need to talk about some other aspect of the meeting first. As always, you must maintain your self-awareness to understand your intention and judge what's best for the situation. A third, very neutral question in that situation would be 'What thoughts are you having about the meeting now?' This may be too vague but, on the other hand, could be just perfect to help them think. Again, your internal sense of what's best to do is one that you need to develop.

At a glance

Your body will help you if you let it!

After many years of coaching others, I've learnt that the following is strange but true.

Your body can often help as an indicator of how a conversation is going, or even act as a guide to suggest what you should do next. During coaching conversations, learn to 'tune in' to your body, particularly your head, stomach and torso, so that you can occasionally check to see how it corresponds to what's happening. For example:

- If the conversation is 'in flow', that is going well, how does your body feel?
- When you know something's not right, how does your body feel?
- When you need to decide, for example, to stay quiet or to speak, how does your body indicate that?

As you gain an increasing awareness of – or connection to – your body, you'll learn to trust and be guided by it. For example, maybe I've been talking to someone about a topic for a while and get a growing sense that the conversation feels 'hollow', or as if the conversation isn't going anywhere. When I check my body, I have a feeling that resonates or is noticeable in some way. Perhaps there's lightness in my stomach or shoulders, or maybe the top of my head feels odd. Or maybe I'll consider asking a certain question, but my stomach feels heavy when I think about it, so I'll stay quiet. These are just a few of my signals – how your body communicates with you will be distinct to you. These body signals are a way to tap into your natural intuition and really boost your coaching ability. Your awareness may take a little time to grow until you can fully trust your senses, but it will make a positive difference to your efficiency and results as a coach.

Behaviour 3: Summarise what you've heard

When you give a short summary of what someone has said it can be helpful for the person you are listening to, and for you, as below.

For you, giving a summary helps you to:

● Demonstrate that you've understood the key points of what someone has said, and so confirm mutual understanding.

● Draw the other person's attention to what you are suggesting are the key facts of the situation, and to filter out any less relevant facts simply by not mentioning them.

● Stay involved in the conversation; for example, as perhaps someone has been talking for a long time without interruption.

For the other person, offering them a summary helps to:

● Give them a rest from talking and space to reflect on what they've been saying.

● Enable them to stand back and listen to their situation from your perspective and so gain a more objective view of key facts or events.

● Become more conscious and aware of the conversation, perhaps as they have digressed in some way and have gotten lost talking about something less important or less relevant.

The benefit of offering a quick summary might surprise you; when someone hears what they've just said, they often have ideas or insight they might not have had otherwise.

> The benefit of offering a quick summary might surprise you

At a glance

Summaries: When less is more

Giving summaries can be so delightfully beneficial that we can overuse it as a tool. In conversation, too many summaries slow progress and potentially frustrate the person who is trying to talk. The following points suggest when a summary might be appropriate:

- When you haven't spoken for a long time and you're experiencing a sense of becoming disconnected from the person talking, for example, they've lost eye contact with you and seem to be talking almost to themselves.

- When you feel that the conversation is rambling or going around in circles, that is the same or similar facts seem to be being repeated.

- When you're unclear as to what you're hearing and want to check that you understand what the other person is saying or feeling.

- When you think that the other person is becoming fatigued or confused and might appreciate a rest from talking, or benefit from some time to reflect.

- When you particularly want to draw the other person's attention to something they've said, for example, a word, phrase or sentiment.

Behaviour 4: Make an observation

An observation is when you notice something, for example what the other person has said, and choose to draw their attention to it. It has a more directive influence than a summary because you have a clear reason for drawing their attention to it. Perhaps they have contradicted themselves in an interesting way, or maybe they've been using a certain phrase or negative language repeatedly and appear unaware of doing that.

When you give an observation, it's good to check first how subjective or objective your observation is. When your observations are more subjective, that is they contain more of your interpretation or opinion, they become more directive, as the following table illustrates.

Observation	Objective or subjective?
You've mentioned three times that the meeting on Monday might be difficult, or tough in some way.	This is factual and allows the other person to judge the importance or relevance.
You seem to be dreading the meeting on Monday.	This is your observation that interprets their feelings behind what they've been saying.
The meeting on Monday seems to be more important to this conversation than the original topic you wanted to discuss.	This is more interpretation by you and clearly, more directive of what you think should happen next.

There are no right or wrong examples here; any of the above may be valid choices, depending on your situation and what seems helpful for the other person.

Behaviour 5: Offer your opinion

When you give an opinion you draw upon your own thoughts, knowledge and experience to offer *your* view of someone else's situation. This is more directive than a summary or an observation, as you have judged the situation and are trying to influence someone else's view or decisions. Be aware that some opinions are more forceful than others, and the impact of giving that opinion relies on:

● your sound judgement of a situation

● the level of rapport/trust you have with the other person

● someone's appetite or potential to hear your opinion and be open to it.

The table below illustrates this.

Your opinion	Strength of 'directiveness' or risk of rejection
'I wonder if Lexi might be a little uncomfortable with her role on the project'.	This is subtly worded to be almost a question to ponder rather than an opinion. Depending on the individual and the situation, this may be useful, or easily ignored!
'I think Lexi sounds like she's uncomfortable with her role on the project'.	This is simple, clear and to the point; it's 'owned' as an opinion, that is 'I think'.
'Lexi's clearly very uncomfortable with her role on the project'.	This is more assertive, pointed and so 'directive' or suggesting of action.

Ideas to action

Develop flexibility by trying something different

To highlight the different ways to influence in conversation, I've described a range of behaviours (see Fig 8.2). You will already use many of these behaviours, often without noticing. For example, I'd guess that you naturally give opinions, advice and instruction but rarely summarise or offer simple observations to help someone else think. To develop true flexibility, try the following.

- First, increase your self-awareness by noticing how you typically influence in conversation or ask a colleague to observe you, for example in meetings.

- Next, decide on a period of time during which you will avoid using your typical behaviours, such as giving opinions or advice, and force yourself to use other responses, such as summarising or making observations. It's often helpful to share with a trusted colleague what you intend to do (this emphasises your commitment).

- Finally, notice the difference this makes, perhaps ask a colleague for feedback; for example 'Did this work? What difference does it make?'

When you've tried using the new behaviours, such as summaries, silence or making objective observations, decide for yourself which behaviours will most benefit you. Remember, the aim of doing this is to influence people in a way that helps them think and act for themselves. So, when you're reviewing ('Does this work?') you need to notice if you did that – or not!

Behaviour 6: Give advice

When you give advice, you tell the other person what you think they should do and accept that they might not actually do it. This is much the same as you might do with a friend, for example, 'If I were you . . . ' or 'What I would do is . . . ' Advice is different from opinion because there is a more open intention to affect the behaviour of another person. To be an effective coach, you should give advice sparingly and with caution. As you already know, coaching leans away from telling people what they should or could do in favour of helping them to think through a situation and decide for themselves.

In the early days of learning to coach, I encourage you to avoid giving advice; instead, develop your ability to be less directive. However, it's also true that there are times when your advice is relevant, useful and supportive and so is exactly what's needed in the situation. The table below will help you reflect on the different 'strengths' of advice, from allowing someone to retain self-direction to giving someone clear instructions.

Your advice	Level of 'directiveness'
'I wonder if you might benefit from a conversation with the HR department'.	This is subtly worded and offers the advice as something that can easily be rejected.
'I think you should go and speak to the HR department'.	This is simple, clear and to the point; it is also owned, that is 'I think'.
'It's really important that you speak to the HR department and get some expert input here'.	This is assertive and pointed, and so is 'directive' or suggesting of action.

Please remember that if you are a person's manager or boss any advice from you may feel like an instruction to them. Your subordinates might expect, or feel that they need, instructions or solutions from you. If you can see this is the case with some people you work with, please put advice in the same category as instruction, because they create the same directive effect on those people. Another option might be to signal that the advice isn't instruction, for example, 'This is just gentle advice – you must decide what's best for you here.'

At a glance

A demonstration of flexible influence (plus how to deal with a bad idea)

Encouraging someone to be self-directed doesn't mean that you need to let them do whatever they want, regardless of the potential consequence. As you develop your flexible style of influence, you can 'pull and push' on the directive lever of influence as the situation warrants. The following dialogue illustrates this.

Manager	So, what do we need to do to win this guy's business?
Javid	I'd like to offer them a bigger discount. I know we'd get the business if we do that.
Manager	[OBSERVATION] Well, yes, that might increase our chances, but we're pretty much down as low as we can go on price. So, a bigger discount isn't an option, I'm afraid.
Javid	Okay, I didn't realise that. What do you think we should do then?
Manager	I think I'm interested to understand what other ideas you can come up with. After all, you have a good relationship with him. Okay, so apart from the price, what else might be important to him?

Here our manager rejects an unfeasible idea by observing why it's not possible. Then, the manager avoids the temptation to offer a solution (and so direct Javid's actions). Instead, the manager challenges Javid to keep thinking/working, that is 'what else is important to him?'

If you consider this from the viewpoint of our Steppingstones Model, (Fig. 8.2) the manager has begun in a less directive position of 'asking', moved to a more directive behaviour of 'make an observation', and then switched direction back to 'asking' – that's what I mean by flexibility of influence.

Behaviour 7: Give an instruction

As you'd expect, when you instruct someone to do something, you aim to influence them by directive means. Interestingly, some instructions are stronger than others. Some instructions prescribe specific, detailed actions, while other 'instructions' tell people how best to work things out for themselves. So, you can use directive instruction to help someone to be self-directed! The table below explains this apparent contradiction.

The instruction	Directive or encourages self-direction?
Go and speak to Jana and ask her to reschedule the meeting.	Clearly, a directive instruction (or request), suggests that you know what should happen and that you are telling someone to do that.
Go and speak to Jana and figure out a solution that you both agree on, and then let me know what you want to do.	Although this is a directive instruction, it still allows the other person a level of empowerment – to decide for themselves what they are going to do.
Okay, take the rest of the day to figure out a solution to this. Get back to me by the end of the day and let me know what you're proposing to do.	This is clearly directive and yet expects the other person to provide a solution. It may put the person under some pressure, which may or may not work well.

Please remember that the above statements can have different effects depending on your manner and tone of voice. For example, a harsh, punchy, snappy tone has a far different impact from a warmer, relaxed one. Try saying the above statements out loud using different styles of speech to explore this idea for yourself.

In a nutshell

A flexible style of influence

It's both unnatural and impractical for your coaching conversations to be merely a list of questions from you, where you allow other people to decide what to do and how to do it. As a manager, you need to be able to balance empowering people with a need to stay practical, within the rules, and so on. This means that you need to develop the flexibility to use different methods of influence, with different people and at different points in a conversation. This includes changing style at any point, for example to switch from being more directive, back to less directive. Being able to use intermediate behaviours, such as giving summaries, making observations, and offering opinions, will help you do this.

CHAPTER 9

How to give constructive feedback

Our fifth and final skill is the ability to give constructive feedback, this is a critical skill for any manager or leader and so I intend to offer some fresh perspectives on the topic. I'll also cover what we mean by constructive feedback in the context of coaching, the principles you need to work from to give someone feedback, and some of the natural barriers you might encounter. As usual, I'll offer hints, tips and guidance, as well as some exercises to build your skills in this area.

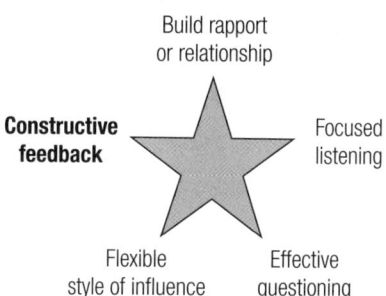

If you are more interested in the stages and sequence of a feedback conversation, then go straight to Chapter 11 and look for 'The Genesis Project' section. There you'll find a worked example of a feedback process that includes dialogue.

What do we mean by feedback?

In the workplace, feedback refers to perspectives, information and opinion given to someone to support their performance, learning and development. For example, I've just given a presentation and you tell me your view of that – what worked, didn't work, and so on. Or perhaps I've worked for you for six months now and you want to have a general conversation about how things are going and offer helpful opinions from your perspective.

Feedback has a poor reputation

Sometimes, in the workplace, the term 'feedback' is used to disguise a piece of criticism. In its worst form, it may even be an act of aggression, if we use the polite term of feedback to 'have a go' at someone. The phrase 'I'd like to give you some feedback' can provoke feelings of doubt or dread in the person about to receive that feedback. That's because they probably imagine they are in trouble, or they are about to be criticised in some way. It's a shame because feedback can be the opposite of that – as I hope to demonstrate.

 Pause and reflect

What do you feel about feedback?

Use the following questions to identify your beliefs about feedback. Allow your mind to wander and imagine the scenarios fully.

Q Imagine a colleague approaches you and says, 'Have you got a few minutes? I'd like to give you some feedback.' How would you feel?

Q Identify someone you work with who might benefit from receiving feedback about something. Now imagine that you've decided to give them that feedback. What do you imagine happening?

Q In either of the above examples, did you imagine that any of the feedback messages might be positive?

Finally, take a little time to reflect on how your beliefs about feedback may affect your ability both to give it and to receive it.

Is it worse to give than to receive?

Many of us dislike giving feedback even more than receiving it. We imagine the potential negative response of the person we're giving feedback to, and that feels uncomfortable. We may also imagine that the person receiving the feedback will think badly of us or reject us for having given them feedback. We might also be concerned that they will get emotional, perhaps defensive, hostile or upset.

> Many of us dislike giving feedback even more than receiving it

Don't think about the blue rabbit

Ironically, our mental preparation for things going badly actually increases the chances of their going badly. That's because our mind draws us towards what we think most about. For example, if I tell you *not* to think about a blue rabbit wearing sunglasses (no, *don't* think about the blue rabbit, the one wearing sunglasses), isn't that just what you think about?

So, before we give feedback, we often use our creative genius to invent nightmarish scenarios and then try to have them 'not' happen. But then, just like telling ourselves *not* to think about the blue rabbit, that's what we focus on. For example, you're preparing to have a conversation with a chatterbox in your team, called Zoe. She's really quite loud, with a laugh you find irritating. As you're preparing to have the conversation you're thinking: 'When I'm telling her about her behaviour, don't say 'shrieking', 'irritating' or 'cackle' – that would sound too personal. Definitely not 'shrieking' or 'cackle' – that would be terrible.' Then, when you have the conversation with Zoe and she asks you to describe what you mean, aren't they the *only* words you can think of?

Solution: focus on what you want

There's a simple solution to this issue: when giving feedback, focus on what you want, instead of what you don't want. For example, in your conversation with Zoe, if you want to use words like 'bubbly, talkative and enthusiastic', think about those words. Put your attention on how you want things to be; it's a simple switch that can alter your course in a conversation dramatically. It works for feelings too. Perhaps you decide you want to feel calm as you give feedback, so think, 'Okay, I'm going to feel calm and relaxed now.' Then build that idea further: think about what it's like to feel calm and relaxed and how that's going to be in the situation. For example: 'Right, I can imagine myself feeling calm and relaxed as I'm talking to her. I can imagine things going well.' As you focus on how things will be when they go well, then you will automatically draw yourself closer to that outcome.

> When giving feedback, focus on what you want, instead of what you don't want

What's fabulous about feedback?

By shifting our attention to what's good about effective feedback and how much value it can be to people, not only do we immediately feel better about it, but we also increase our chances of giving feedback that others value. Here are just a few of the positive benefits of giving your colleagues at work constructive feedback.

- People appreciate that you're committed to and supportive of their development (especially when they think you've made a real effort to give it).

- We often enjoy talking about ourselves, especially when it helps us to get better at something. Imagine your manager never bothered to tell you how you were doing – how would that feel?

- We relish learning. We want to feel as though we're making progress in an area, especially where it's a personal challenge that we feel is worthwhile.

What are the key principles of feedback?

Most of the principles that follow relate to messages that can be either 'positive' or 'negative'. Both of those terms are subjective. For example, you receive feedback that you seem to place more importance on completing tasks than on how people are feeling; I might call that message negative, but you might find it positive. So, let's assume that by positive we mean complimentary statements, and by negative we mean more difficult messages about a problem or a need to improve. In either case, the following principles work, especially when giving messages that feel difficult in some way.

Preparation: why, what, how

Before you give feedback, first make sure that you prepare and focus on a positive outcome. For example, why do you want to give feedback and what are the messages you want to give? How and where will you deliver your messages? Also, think a little about how the other person is likely to respond, that is how

> It often works to drop the use of the word 'feedback' completely

they might feel. Consider the other person and the situation and decide the best way to approach them. For example, it often works to drop the use of the word 'feedback' completely, perhaps saying instead 'Can we have a chat about the meeting yesterday? I'd like to talk about how that went.'

For a fuller list of preparation points, see the checklist later in this chapter.

Feeling buoyant, staying 'above zero'

During any conversation, your emotional state either helps or hinders your ability to think, speak and react resourcefully. Let's imagine that there's a range of emotional states that we might place at different points on a numbered scale. Anything above zero is generally positive – for example calm, relaxed and confident – and zero is neutral. Below zero might be more negative feelings of hesitation, trepidation or even annoyance and frustration. I encourage you to give feedback only when you are

> Give feedback only when you are feeling emotionally balanced

feeling emotionally balanced, or even after you've cultivated a sense of optimism about the situation (especially if you're delivering a tough message). Your emotional balance also influences the person you are talking to and will support them to receive the messages you are offering.

At a glance

Build your confidence and then give feedback

If you are finding it difficult to reach 'above zero', for example, to feel calm and focused, try some or all of the following.

- Go for a walk to think things through - settle your mind through the combination of movement and reflection.
- Decide how you want to feel and focus on that feeling - use your breathing and posture to help with that. For example, if you want to feel confident then walk confidently, breathe and adopt the physical posture of how you typically are when you're feeling relaxed and confident.
- Focus on a positive outcome - imagine the conversation going well and see yourself as you want to be. See, hear and feel what that will be like.

- Get a trusted colleague to help you prepare – either talk things through or, better still, rehearse. Rehearsal is a proven method of ironing out any creases in a planned conversation.

- Consider not giving the feedback – just allow yourself to imagine that you don't give the feedback after all. Does that feel better or not? Is your relief temporary or lasting? If you decide not to give the feedback, ask yourself – have you decided to do the right thing or just the easy thing? That way you'll know if your decision is good enough for you.

Give feedback with positive intention

Constructive feedback is given with a positive intention for the person receiving it. For example, you might intend that your messages benefit their personal growth, progress on a task or their performance at work generally. Of course, there may be other reasons that feel less positive, for example, they have behaved in a negative way towards someone, and you want to avoid that

> Rehearsal is a proven method of ironing out any creases in a planned conversation

happening again. To frame the conversation with the person you intend to give feedback to, first, please consider your intentions towards them. Are they positive? Consider giving the feedback, then ask yourself: 'How might the other person benefit?'

Once you're clear about what the benefit might be for the individual, if it's appropriate, you can share that benefit with them. For example, 'I'm hoping this might take some of the pressure off you in the team meetings.' If your motivation for giving feedback seems to be based on your emotional state, for example, 'I'm really annoyed with them' or 'I just don't like them as a person', then you need to reflect further and find an objective viewpoint to guide you. If you are unable to find this neutral view, you are less likely to be able to speak objectively (and remain impartial) during the conversation.

Own your own message, say what is true for you

If your reason for giving feedback is that someone else thinks it's a good idea, I'd suggest caution. For example, Niamh works for you and is complaining about Bharat, who also works for you. Niamh complains that on the days that you're not in the office, Bharat shows up late and she'd like you to tackle him about it. While you have no reason to doubt Niamh is telling the truth (you trust her), this is not a huge issue with you personally. Bharat is one of the stronger-performing members of the team. The only real issue is that Niamh feels the situation is unfair and expects you, as manager, to ensure that 'fairness reigns'. Your issue is more of a question of integrity. For example, do you try to calm Niamh down about this, in the hope that the issue goes away? Or do you have a conversation with Bharat and risk creating a real issue? After all, Bharat may feel aggrieved that someone has complained about him and be suspicious of the whole team if the individual isn't open about it. Or Bharat may reject accusations against him as untrue, in which case it will be very difficult to make progress – unless Niamh speaks up.

> Feedback is normally best owned by and attributed to the person with the issue

Feedback is normally best owned by and attributed to the person with the issue. One valid option is to encourage Niamh to offer feedback herself. Explain your reasons and the risks of your giving feedback to Bharat in this situation. In exceptional circumstances, that is where you simply cannot avoid giving a message, then you have the option of acting as a mediator in the situation. For example, 'I'm having this conversation on behalf of Rory because he doesn't feel able to raise it with you personally.' Rory needs to know that you're doing this, and both Rory and the person you're giving feedback to need to be encouraged to stay constructive afterwards. This might mean that you facilitate a conversation between them or encourage them to talk things through in a constructive way.

Stay objective (avoid subjective opinion)

Staying objective means that we strip out as much of our own personal judgement as possible and instead use the observable facts of a situation. Subjective statements contain our interpretation, for example what we think. Subjective statements rely on the accuracy of our judgement and can more easily be rejected or refuted. Objective statements tend to be more neutral, as they are more accurate and so more easily accepted.

Let's assume that you've decided to give a colleague called Markus some feedback about his tendency to make commitments and then not keep them. It's important to give this message in an objective, not subjective, way; the statements in the table below illustrate this.

Subjective statement	Objective statement
I'm not sure if you're coping or not – I just get the feeling that you're not.	Our last couple of update conversations have seemed to be mostly about things that are being delivered late.
You don't deliver things when you say you're going to – it makes a mockery of our planning process, and yesterday was a disaster.	I've had some experiences recently where I've had to chase you for things you said you'd deliver – the missing data yesterday has caused us to push out the dates on our plan.

As you can see, the objective statements seem more factual. Perhaps the terms 'mostly' or 'some experiences' are a little vague and the actual number might work better, for example 'two experiences this week'. However, to give a lighter message I've not used the actual amount. Remember, we want to progress the conversation towards a solution, rather than simply pointing out someone's wrongdoings. For a better idea of the structure and stages of a constructive feedback conversation, see Chapter 11 ('The Genesis project' example).

At a glance

Prepare to give feedback

Before you next give someone feedback, take a few moments to consider the following.

- Why do you want to give feedback – how might it benefit the other person?
- Is this your own feedback or someone else's – can you 'own' the messages?
- What are the key messages you want to give – are they objective and based on behaviour?
- How, where and when do you plan to give the messages – are the timing and situation appropriate?
- How are you feeling about giving the feedback – are you 'above zero' emotionally?
- What are the outcomes that you hope to achieve from the conversation?
- How might the person receiving the observations react to this feedback?

Once you've given feedback, you might like to reflect on how well it went, or what you might want to do differently next time. If you're feeling brave, you might even ask the person to whom you gave the feedback for some feedback!

Comment on behaviour, not personality

Constructive feedback comments on behaviour rather than the person or their personality. For example, 'You're overbearing' attacks the person, whereas 'Sometimes you talk over people' comments on their behaviour. Generally, we feel we have a choice about what we do but have much less choice about who we are. So, give messages based on observations of behaviour, rather than judgements of the person or their personality. The table below gives further examples.

Comments on person	Comments on behaviour
You're rubbish at keeping commitments.	Sometimes you don't keep your commitments.
I find you controlling.	I'd like you to listen to my ideas more often.
You're stubborn.	I'd encourage you to respond more flexibly sometimes.

Give a balanced message

Aim to give balanced messages where appropriate and offer positives with negatives. But only do that if the positives relate to the negatives in some way, and you can deliver the positives in a *genuine, natural way*. By natural, I mean in a way that feels natural for the conversation, in flow with what's being discussed. The following example comes part-way through a conversation with Tanya after her manager has told her that, in meetings, Tanya voices her own ideas with great passion and conviction and often ignores or interrupts the input of others.

Manager   Tanya, I'll add that I do value your energy
in these meetings – you're able to get everyone behind a situation, which is great –
it's just that sometimes some of the quieter
members of the team seem less able to offer
ideas, and if possible, I'd like to gain their
input on these things.

The manager has balanced the negative point with a positive
acknowledgement (that they value Tanya's energy) while not
detracting from the main message. We aim to acknowledge positive attributes and behaviours where
it's appropriate. By doing so, we create a sense of perspective on a situation and help the person receiving
feedback remain buoyant. What works
much less well is when we try to think of something positive and
put it into the conversation in a phoney attempt to 'prop up' a
bleak message. So, keep positive messages genuine!

> Acknowledge positive
> attributes and behaviours
> where it's appropriate

At a glance

Encourage more desirable behaviour: Go towards a solution

It's often more helpful to tell someone what you'd prefer rather than
what you don't like. For example, 'Don't talk so much' becomes
'Listen to other people's ideas more often'. It helps someone to focus
on the solution, rather than get 'stuck' in the problem. It's a subtle
switch, but one that has a real impact.

Check for understanding and engagement

It helps to understand what someone is taking from the feedback
message, that is what they have actually heard and understood.
You also want some initial sense of how engaged or motivated

they are to create change as a result. There's also a benefit in keeping them involved in the conversation (rather than only listening to you talk). To reduce pressure from someone, keep your questions deliberately vague, to enable someone to enter the conversation, without feeling they need to answer in any specific way. It may be as simple as asking 'How does this sound?' or 'What are your thoughts about this?'

Creating dialogue (rather than a lecture) is a good way to maintain rapport and help your messages to be effective. When we check for understanding and engagement, we also take the pressure off ourselves to talk, as we help the other person to offer their views or responses. The key is to remember to do it at an appropriate point, that is after you have given your feedback message. The following example comes part-way through the meeting with Tanya again, just after the manager has described her tendency to talk over people in meetings.

Manager	So basically, it's about the impact this has on others, and also possibly the overall balance of conversation in the meeting. Can I ask what your thoughts about this are?
Tanya	Well, I guess I'm a bit taken aback by it, I mean I didn't realise it was an issue. I certainly didn't think that other people might stay quiet just because of what I'm saying.
Manager	Right. [neutral tone followed by silence].
Tanya	I mean, you just expect that if people have something to say then they say it – I know that's what I do. Why can't they do that?

So, the manager is giving Tanya a chance to express herself and process some of her reactions to the feedback. Her initial reactions may not be her final response, and so the manager doesn't react to them. Instead, the manager uses silence to allow Tanya to voice her immediate thoughts. But if the manager had simply kept talking, explaining the situation, and leaving Tanya no room to respond, then Tanya may feel suppressed in the conversation. As a coaching manager, you operate from a position of equality with the people you manage. So, it's important that this is a conversation between two adults, rather than a 'parent-to-child' reprimand.

> That this is a conversation between two adults, rather than a 'parent-to-child' reprimand

Help them decide on a way forward

To maintain an 'adult-to-adult' conversation, it's best if actions or next steps are agreed upon in collaboration, rather than you simply instructing them as their manager. Helping someone else to decide will allow them to engage with what they feel is a good way forward that works for them. You're obviously free to offer views on their decisions, but please be cautious. Sometimes it's better to let someone proceed with what you think is a flawed plan rather than dismiss their plan in favour of your own. After all, most situations can be given time to evolve further, so you don't need to find what *you* think is a perfect solution. Your own wisdom will help you to decide when to challenge and when to let go.

The following example continues the previous scenario and offers an appropriate balance from the manager in terms of challenge and 'letting go'.

Manager	So, having thought a little about this now, what are your options, do you think?
Tanya	Well, I'm tempted just to stay quiet, and then no one can say I'm not letting anyone else speak!

Manager	Well, it's an option, but given that I really value your input, it's probably not great long-term. What else could you do?
Tanya	Well, I don't know – be more aware of others I suppose. I mean, I'm certainly going to think about it. I just need to realise when others have something to say.
Manager	Okay, how do you see that working?
Tanya	I guess I need to learn to stop talking a bit more quickly or get to the point quicker. I'm not sure – I'm going to have to think about this.
Manager	I think it sounds like you're on the right track, and, yes, you'd want to think about it, wouldn't you? I'm not sure it takes any more than that.

The manager is again using a very light touch in the conversation. They don't need to prescribe a list of agreed actions, for example, talk to other people, write an email, and so on. The manager knows that this is an issue of self-awareness first, which will need some reflection time. They also trust that Tanya is engaged with the topic and wants to do something about it. The manager is assuming that Tanya is a mature adult and will work on this issue afterwards. They also know that if her behaviour remains the same, then they can revisit the topic and can do so on a firmer footing.

After this, all the manager needs to do is close the conversation in a way that demonstrates ongoing support and commitment.

Manager	Tanya, I'm wondering what support you might need from me for this.
Tanya	[pauses] Nothing right now – maybe there might be something later, but right now it's fine.
Manager	Okay, good. Well, let me know. So, are we all right to leave this here?

So, the manager has offered some initial feedback and left it with Tanya to reflect and then act on, while leaving the topic open for future debate. If the manager sees a continuation of the issue, they can simply revisit the conversation. Conversely, if the manager sees improvements, then they'll want to acknowledge those in a genuine way. With these acknowledgements of progress, Tanya can view what might have been an uncomfortable conversation as actually one that was really valuable to her.

In a nutshell

Constructive feedback

Constructive, supportive feedback supports us to learn, develop and succeed; most of us would choose to receive it fairly regularly. So, the ability to give helpful, motivating feedback is a necessary tool for any effective manager. To do that, your challenge is to offer your messages in a balanced, natural style so that people can welcome and engage with them. And if you want to develop as a manager with a coaching style, that is one who accelerates the development and learning of others, then it's important that you give regular, constructive feedback.

PART 3

Application

I n this part of the book, we'll look at the different ways you might use coaching in your workplace. We'll look at coaching conversations that you plan to have, as well as coaching as a natural response to everyday questions or situations. To help you link principles to actual behaviour, you'll find structures of conversation as well as sample dialogue.

Rather than reading this part front to back, it can be read selectively, to suit your needs. I've given you four different scenarios in which coaching might happen, to show you how coaching fits within each one. All the basic coaching principles discussed so far stay the same; it's just your objectives for having the conversation that might be slightly different. Before you decide how much you want to read, please first familiarise yourself with what type of circumstance each scenario caters for. That way you can start with what's most relevant to you and pick up on the other scenarios as you need them. It's a little like a recipe book – you can flick through and see what you fancy, and what most suits you right now. And of course, you can revisit any scenario in the future, as a guide for a particular situation when it crops up.

You'll find a summary of what each scenario does below. First, let me explain how coaching occurs in the workplace.

Where and when can you coach?

Coaching principles work in a variety of situations and it's useful to highlight the differences between those situations, as the structures that support them can be slightly different. By structure, I simply mean the sequence of activities that build your conversational journey. For example, if you have regular one-to-one update meetings with subordinates, I'll offer a simple structure called The Coaching Path to help you navigate that conversation. If, however, you're in a busy work environment and want to coach more 'in the moment', then your approach will be different. So, I'll also offer you a reduced structure for those bite-sized conversations, that is where your coaching conversations may last 60 seconds or less. I call this shorter structure Response Coaching.

Planned or unplanned – a useful distinction

I'll use the terms 'unplanned' and 'planned' to describe coaching conversations in the heart of the action or away from it. For example, if we are at our desks engaged in the task of reading emails, checking reports and so on. and someone approaches us with a question that turns into a coaching exchange, that's an unplanned activity. However, if we leave our desks and go to a meeting room for a scheduled update with a subordinate, that's a planned conversation. Both terms are imperfect as some activities appear one way but may actually be another, for example, if someone approaches unexpectedly and gives you a fairly formal set-up, for example 'I wonder if I could get your advice on something, it's kind of a priority issue, do you have time for a conversation right now?', then you may decide to use the more formal structure of The Coaching Path to deal with that (even though this conversation is unplanned). For now, let's assume that when we use the terms 'planned' and 'unplanned', it's the difference between situations where you are expecting to coach someone, and when your coaching is just an instinctive response to a quick question or an unforeseen conversation.

Where do you want to start coaching?

Now all you need to decide are the situations in which you want to start to use coaching principles and behaviours. Use the following descriptions to choose which scenario most closely matches the type of coaching you might want to do first.

Chapter 10: Planned session when the individual has the topic or agenda

This scenario is a scheduled meeting with a subordinate, where you want them to 'own' the session and be responsible for setting the objectives and desired outcome. Ideally, they will come prepared with an idea of what they want to get from their time with you. And if they don't, you'll simply help them work out what they want to get from the meeting in the first few minutes. This scenario enables you to imagine more 'pure coaching' from you as a manager, as your subordinate is encouraged to be responsible right from the start. I'll use The Coaching Path to guide you through this conversation.

Chapter 11: Planned session when the manager has the topic or agenda

If you're looking to learn how to give constructive feedback in a coaching style – this is the one. Here, I'll demonstrate a conversation about someone's performance, where you want to give constructive feedback (which will include some tougher messages or areas for development). This is a meeting or conversation with a subordinate where you, as the manager, 'own' the agenda, that is you know what you want to get from the meeting and want to adopt a coaching style during that. As a support structure, this scenario also uses The Coaching Path.

So, in this example, the manager initiates the conversation and knows what they want to get from it, for example, raising an issue or encouraging change. As the manager here, your challenge is to coach and facilitate the conversation and be less directive. To create a collaborative session (rather than a reprimand) you'll want to engage the subordinate in the conversation as soon as possible.

Chapter 12: Planned session when both the individual and the manager have things to discuss

This is a meeting with a colleague or subordinate where the subordinate has objectives for the conversation and so do you. As a manager, your agenda here relates to your areas of interest or work priority (not giving tough messages or constructive feedback). For example, 'I'd like an update on how the conference arrangements are going'. By blending the principles of the previous two scenarios, we can flex between the two. This scenario also uses the supporting structure of The Coaching Path.

Chapter 13: Unplanned conversation – Response Coaching in a live environment

This scenario shows how coaching occurs as a natural behavioural response by a manager in a busy work environment. When faced with quick questions, issues or even complaints, managers can choose to coach issues rather than fix them. Using the Response Coaching model, coaching becomes as easy as one, two, three. If you're managing a busy team and frequently get asked questions, or are expected to solve problems, this scenario is for you!

CHAPTER 10

Planned conversation: When the individual has the topic or agenda

et's imagine that one of your team wants to talk to you about something and they want to do it away from the workplace. Perhaps they have an issue or are bothered about a situation and want to discuss this with you. It may be something apparently trivial, like a minor concern about a deadline, or something more significant, such as a crisis of confidence. It can be a fairly brief conversation, for example, 20 minutes, or something that lasts much longer, perhaps an hour or more. So what follows is simply a conversation that is anticipated by you, for example because this has been scheduled or agreed upon in advance.

The Coaching Path

For all planned scenarios, we're going to use one basic structure, The Coaching Path. This is illustrated in Figure 10.1.

While The Coaching Path has five stages, the first and last stages will already be familiar to you. These stages are simply about the beginning and end of a conversation. We'll explain these, in brief, to make sure you feel comfortable about opening and closing the session. The key stages that distinguish this conversation as a coaching conversation are the middle three stages, which we'll cover a little more thoroughly.

Let's now use The Coaching Path to help you navigate a planned coaching conversation.

The Coaching Path

Establish conversation	• Introduce session • 'How are you?' etc. • Create coaching climate/atmosphere
Identify topic and goal	• 'What would you like to talk about?' • 'What do you want to get from this?' • 'What do we need to do in this conversation?'
Enquiry understanding/insight	• 'Tell me about the situation.' • 'What's been happening?' • Summaries, reflection, challenge, etc.
Shape conclusions/agreements	• 'So what are you thinking of doing?' • 'What are your options?' • 'What have you decided?'
Completion/close	• 'Let's just confirm...' • 'Has that been useful?' • 'Are we complete?'

Figure 10.1 The Coaching Path

At a glance

Planned: Key coaching principles

Here's a quick reminder of the key principles that support a planned coaching conversation in this context.

● This is an 'adult-to-adult' conversation, that is you are both mature and equal in the conversation.

● The other person is responsible both for the issue they are surfacing and for their actions in relation to that issue – not in a 'blame' sense, but simply because they are empowered to think and act.

● The other person owns the agenda, that is they know what they want to discuss and also what they want to get out of the meeting.

● The other person often has their own solution to the situation or can be challenged to create a way forward for themselves.

- You add value to the conversation by facilitating their thoughts and ideas, using effective questioning to provoke thought and offering your observations and feedback.

- Although you might have advice you could offer, you prefer that they come up with solutions. You're prepared not to give answers until it becomes silly not to. Even then, you'll make 'gentle offers', for example, 'Can I offer a thought?'

Stage 1: Establish conversation

This step is about creating an appropri- ate sense of the conversation, for example, 'We're here to discuss a work- related topic'. Remember, it's a conver- sation of equals, rather than a meeting with the head of school, so think about how to adopt an 'adult-to-adult' pos- ture and tone. Remember the impor- tance of rapport and warmth. You aim to create a relaxed yet professional tone

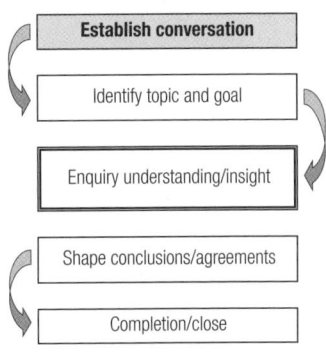

to the conversation that enables the other person to feel comfortable and speak freely. This is balanced with a clear sense that this topic is important to progress efficiently, so you'll create a sense of leader- ship, without being controlling. Your colleague must be comfortable that you can navigate through the stages of the conversation, that is you know what you're doing. That will be clearer as we go along. So, your objectives at this stage include:

- To build appropriate levels of rapport, to help the other person feel comfortable and to encourage natural conversation

- To create the appropriate climate for the conversation, for example, professional warmth

- To create a sense of trust in you, that is they are in safe hands.

The following dialogue begins a planned coaching conversation between Tasha and her manager. As we'll use this conversation to illustrate each stage of The Coaching Path in this chapter, you might like to imagine yourself as the manager.

Manager	So, Tasha, hi, how are you – how are things?
Tasha	Yes, fine thanks, settling in nicely I think.
Manager	How do you like the new layout? You got a spot by the window I see.
Tasha	Yes, it's great, I much prefer it.
Manager	Yes, I think all of us being in one place is great. Good, so, okay, we've got about 30 minutes for this, haven't we?
Tasha	Yes, it might not take that long, but I booked the slot just in case.
Manager	That's fine. Let's get started, shall we?

As you can see, the manager here is simply greeting the team member in an appropriate way, and when it feels natural, moving the conversation on to the task at hand. In all these examples I'll reduce the dialogue as much as possible, to stick to the key points. In real life, your conversation would likely contain more small talk or general chat, but it's less helpful here.

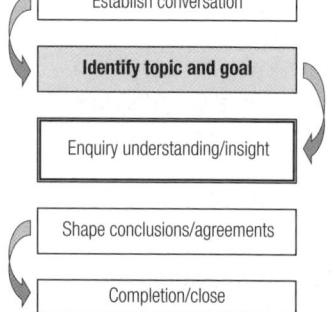

Stage 2: Identify a clear topic and goal

This next stage creates a sense of direction and purpose for the conversation so that as the coach you know where you need to be heading. Remember, we're in a conversation where the colleague/subordinate has the objective for the conversation, so the manager needs to identify the objectives for the conversation from what their colleague says. Your objectives at this stage include:

- To encourage your colleague to 'own' the session by declaring what they want to get from it
- To identify the purpose and topic for the session in sufficient detail to enable you to facilitate the conversation towards an effective outcome
- To establish the conditions of an effective conversation, for example, we'll know when we're on track and when we've wandered into a pointless digression
- To create a sense that 'success is possible' or a 'solution focus', that is we're here to work something out and this is where we will get to
- To identify an 'end point' for the conversation, that is know when you've met the objectives.

Here you are surfacing your colleague's *topic* for discussion and also their *goal* for the conversation. That might be something fairly easy for you to do, for example, if they are well prepared and feeling clear. Or it might be something you need to help them get clear about before you can begin an effective discussion. It's worth mentioning that you have an important balance to maintain at this point. That balance is between being effective and not frustrating the person in front of you, who might be eager to launch into a topic that they want to get off their chest. At this stage, you need a 'star to guide you' rather than a super detailed description of their agenda.

The following dialogue maps the stages between a goal that is too vague and one that has just enough clarity for you to navigate forwards.

| Manager | So, what would you like to talk about? |
| *Tasha* | Well, it's the whole situation with the team and recruitment we've got right now. To be honest, it's beginning to be a real concern. |

So here you have a vague (broad) topic and not much of a goal for the conversation. While Tasha is likely to be ready to begin talking about her 'problem', the manager probably needs to push back a little, and gain a little more focus on the conversation. For example:

| *Manager* | Okay, specifically what is it regarding the team and recruitment you want us to talk about? |
| *Tasha* | Well, it's just the delays we're getting with hiring; it's taking too long to bring people on board and the work is piling up. |

So now we're clearer about the topic for the conversation, but we still have no goal to work towards. Depending on how Tasha seems – for example calm, flustered, frustrated, and so on – you may decide that you need to proceed to the next stage (enquiry and understanding) to allow her to speak. Your risk is that the conversation will simply become a 'complaining session', where Tasha explains the situation to you in the hope that it will simply get resolved in some way (by you perhaps?). So, let's risk a further challenge.

| *Manager* | Right, so that's what we need to work through. Thinking about the next 30 minutes, what do you want to get out of this conversation? |
| *Tasha* | Well, I guess I want to tell you about what's been going on, and maybe get some ideas as to what else I can do. |

Notice how the responsibility for the conversation and its outcome is still firmly with Tasha. The manager is working to maintain rapport and show support – 'That's what we need to work through' – while still encouraging Tasha to own the conversation. For some managers, this will be a challenge, as they may judge this lack of involvement by themselves as unhelpful. In the longer term, it's more helpful to Tasha, as she learns to solve life's problems and feels confident about doing that. As a manager, if at any time you need to step in and rescue someone, you can. Just remember that when you rescue someone you make a victim out of them at the same

> When you rescue someone you make a victim out of them

moment. When we are a victim, we feel less powerful, as if something is happening *to* us. A more powerful posture to act from is the assumption that we are the cause of our experience and can change that experience ourselves. As a manager, you encourage others to adopt a more powerful posture like this by assuming that they are able to make a difference in their circumstances themselves (without the need to be rescued).

Back to our Tasha scenario, now that we have both a topic and a goal for the conversation, we can progress to the next stage: enquiry, understanding and insight.

At a glance

Ask people to arrive prepared

Your regular one-to-one meetings with subordinates are easier to coach when they work from the idea that what they get from those is largely up to them – for example, that they prepare a clear sense of objective or purpose in advance. Ask them to arrive with topics they want to discuss and also some objectives for each topic, or

▶

perhaps even to send you an agenda ahead of the meeting. It's a great way to get people to act more powerfully. When they arrive for a conversation prepared, they also begin with a more mature posture, for example 'Here's what I want to get from my time with you', instead of 'Oh, I thought we'd just chat some stuff through and see what happens'.

Stage 3: Enquiry, understanding and insight

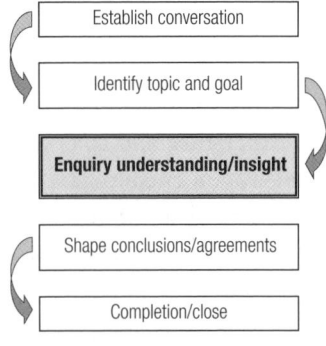

This is perhaps the most important stage in our Coaching Path, as it is where your core coaching skills come into play. It is also the heart of a coaching conversation, where your effective listening, questioning and observations or challenges enable the person to surface their thoughts and arrive at their own conclusions and decisions. The simple process of enquiry, that is being listened to, is also therapeutic as we are given space to get things off our chest and perhaps feel better for having expressed emotions such as confusion or frustration. Your key objectives at this stage are:

● To surface a mutual understanding of the situation, issue or challenge (e.g. what is the issue, what's causing the issue, what's important about the issue?)

● To increase the self-awareness of the individual, in relation to the situation being discussed (e.g. how might they be affecting the situation?)

● To help the other person reflect objectively on the situation (e.g. express confusion or frustration) and then move on to a more impartial, balanced view

- To help them form conclusions, realisations or insights arising from clearer thinking

- To create more of a focus towards a solution (e.g. what would be better than this, or how do you want this situation to be instead?).

In our conversation with Tasha, here's how the process of enquiry might sound. Again, I've reduced the conversation right down to keep it simple to read.

At a glance

Your intention is to understand (not to 'fix')

When, as a manager, we coach, our enquiry has the intention to create mutual understanding rather than to help us fix, solve or instruct the other person. While enquiring merely to understand may seem like a pointless task, it is actually where the magic of coaching reveals itself. When someone is asked to paint a proper picture of their own issue or challenge, they can often think more clearly and rationally as a result. As they speak, they form realisations about the situation and about themselves in relation to that situation. This clarity of perception is likely to lie hidden otherwise. It's as if you declutter someone's thoughts for them – from a clearer perspective they can make more sense of their situation. Sometimes we just need to empty our heads of confused static so that a clear signal can be heard!

Manager	Right, so can you tell me a bit more about the situation?
Tasha	Yes, it's quite straightforward. We sent requests to HR for two new people four weeks ago and so far they haven't even started the first interviews. They're saying they're really busy with the year-end pay reviews. It's ridiculous.

Manager	Okay. How does that impact you and the team?
Tasha	Well, immediately it's not too bad – we've still got Margaret here until the end of the month, but when she leaves, we're really going to feel the pressure.
Manager	Okay, so once Margaret leaves, then what happens?
Tasha	Well, then we've got to find a way of coping with her workload and a way of taking over the new product-report work that's being passed over from Marketing.
Manager	Right, I can see why you'd want to tackle this now before it becomes a real issue.
Tasha	Exactly. It's going to be a mess if we don't do something soon.

As you can see, the manager is gently building the facts of the situation, getting clear and helping Tasha to focus on the key facts. The manager is also demonstrating empathy ('I can see why you'd want to tackle this now') to acknowledge her concern. Let's continue.

Manager	So, what have you already done about this?
Tasha	Well, I've been chasing HR about it, as they seem to hold all the cards. I spoke to them yesterday and they still hadn't set a date for their first interviews.
Manager	First interviews?
Tasha	Yes, they like to do the first round of vetting candidates before they get to us. Once they've seen people, they pass them over to us.

Manager	So where are they in that process?
Tasha	Well, apparently, they've got at least three candidates they think we'd be interested in, but they still haven't arranged to see them.

By now, your problem-solving skills may have leapt into gear and you think you've spotted a solution, that is remove the 'blocking factor' of HR and get Tasha to interview the candidates first. But remember, you are committed to Tasha's ability to come up with her own way forward. Plus, there may be more information you need to hear before you jump to a conclusion.

Manager	Okay, so let me just confirm what I think you're saying: that we need to hire more people quickly, to cope with Margaret leaving at the end of this month, plus to take on the additional work from Marketing.
Tasha	Right.
Manager	HR have some candidates, but they want to vet them first, and they haven't arranged to see them yet.
Tasha	Yes, and if you're thinking why not let us speak to them first, it's because they haven't sat the IQ tests. If the candidate passes the IQ tests, they're then asked to sign a data protection agreement. HR won't let them speak to us until they've signed it.

Notice how the manager uses a gentle summary with a positive effect, before continuing to enquire further. We now have a fuller picture and one that is useful to surface. If the manager had acted on a 'fix-it' instinct earlier, their 'simple solution' (remove HR from the process) may have been rejected as an impractical suggestion. And remember, it's Tasha who will benefit the most by finding her own solution. Let's continue.

Manager	So, what are your options?
Tasha	Well, we could insist on seeing them before HR does and get the candidates to sign the data protection form ourselves, but it still won't get us the people in time. Because even if we said yes to a candidate, getting references and checks on them will still take around a month, maybe longer.
Manager	Hmm, so that's not going to sort it.
Tasha	No – certainly it's not going to keep us covered in the short term.
Manager	Okay, so let me just check, what is the real issue here you need to fix?
Tasha	Well, I suppose there are two different issues, aren't there? There's Margaret leaving and there's the new workload. We can deal with either situation for a short time, but not both at once. For example, if Margaret stayed on for a few weeks we could cope, or if we could push back the new workload coming in from Marketing, we could let her go.
Manager	So, what do you think?
Tasha	Well, I'm thinking I need to look into both of those options, to see what's possible.

As you can see, the conversation has taken a slightly different turn, and now Tasha has got clearer. You'll also notice that the conversation has gone from one with no sense of possibility ('It's a mess') to one with more sense of a potential solution ('I need to see what's possible').

Now that we have a clearer picture of both the issue and Tasha's options, we've fulfilled the enquiry stage of The Coaching Path. So, let's go to the next stage.

At a glance

Don't withhold information (that's not coaching)

While the manager should avoid giving quick solutions, if they know of any information that is relevant to a subordinate's issue then they need to declare it – for example 'Did you realise that Marketing is making people redundant?' We don't want to withhold information; we simply want to reduce our influence on someone's decision-making process. Remember, you can't coach knowledge, that is if someone doesn't know the capital of Bolivia, it's pointless to ask them for that.

Stage 4: Shape conclusions and agreements

Here we want to start to pull the conversation together and help Tasha shape her ideas into an appropriate way forward. In any coaching conversation, the appropriate way forward may range from an agreed set of actions with timescales to a much looser plan of 'go and have a think'. As coach, you can decide on how much rigour and detail to encourage,

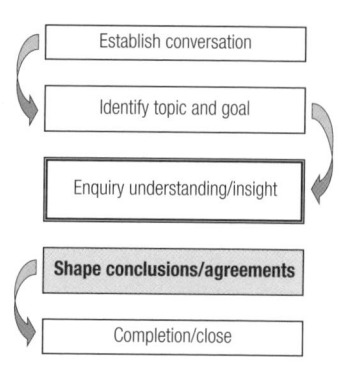

according to both the topic that has been discussed and the individual with whom you are discussing it. For example, when you know the other person is a mature individual able to act upon commitments, then if they say, 'I'm going to go away and look at the figures – I'll get back to you', that may be enough. Or if the topic of the conversation has been highly personal (e.g. 'Am I in the right job?'), then an agreement to 'go away and think' may be very appropriate. But if what you're discussing is time related or you need clarity, then 'I'll come back to you on Friday morning by 9 a.m. with the document' might be needed.

In this fourth stage of shaping conclusions and agreements, your objectives are:

- To provide a useful summary of the point the individual has reached, that is their conclusions and ideas
- To help the individual to surface any remaining conclusions or ideas that are useful
- To help them to decide on a way forward, for example, actions, next steps, and so on.
- To challenge any false barriers or limited thinking
- To create a sense of a better future (e.g., how will this benefit you?) and so motivate the person to act.

Let's continue our scenario with Tasha.

Manager	Okay, let's try to pull this together then. So, you're suggesting that if you split the two issues – Margaret leaving and the impending workload from Marketing – then it may be simpler to deal with.
Tasha	Yes, we can cope with one but not with both, at least for a while.
Manager	Right, and you're going to find out how possible it might be either to keep Margaret on for a while or to delay the new work coming in.
Tasha	Yes, it's certainly worth looking into.
Manager	Yes, I think it probably is. And I guess I'm still left wondering, what are you going to do about the longer-term solution of hiring more people?

Here you'll notice that the manager is happy to support Tasha to pursue the short-term 'fixes' but also wants to challenge the remaining issue of what happens longer term. I'll add that because the manager has been in the role of coach or facilitator for the conversation, this apparent oversight is actually very easy to spot. Because the manager hasn't been trying to 'figure things out' or create ideas, they are able to maintain a much clearer view of the conversation. Let's see how this continues.

Tasha	Yes, I know, I really need to get to grips with those guys, don't I?
Manager	[laughs] Probably – what are you thinking of doing?
Tasha	Well, for a start I need them to commit to some firm deadlines. I do think there's an option for us to see people first – we can do the data protection form, and we can even arrange the meetings ourselves if we have to.
Manager	What difference will that make, do you think?
Tasha	At a minimum, we'll tighten the whole process. If we're successful, we'll probably shave around three or four weeks off the hiring period.
Manager	How will HR react, do you think?
Tasha	Well, if I can do it in the right way, I think they'll welcome me with open arms.
Manager	The right way?
Tasha	[laughs] Yes, you know, make it look like I'm taking something off their plate during a very busy period or something!
Manager	[smiling] Ah, I'm sure you'll charm them into an agreement.

Again, you can see the manager is using a 'light touch' to help Tasha plan her own way forward. In reality, the manager may decide that for the sake of clarity they want to summarise the three actions (Margaret, Marketing and HR), or indeed offer further challenges or observations. But for the purposes of this example, let's assume the manager is comfortable that Tasha has her way forward. We're ready to go to the final stage: completion and close.

At a glance

What if someone gets 'stuck' when you ask them for solutions or ideas?

First, stay calm, relaxed and focused and use your breathing to stay calm and centred. Your best response to someone who appears stuck will depend on what's causing their 'block'. It could be several reasons:

● They need reflection time – a period of gentle silence helps.

● They need a more general question, for example, 'What are your options?' or 'What thoughts are you having now?'

● They are confused or overloaded. A gentle summary from you can give them a 'rest'. In extreme cases, offer them a break or even reschedule.

● You haven't surfaced enough information yet. Backtrack – for example, 'Okay, I've heard you say that long hours, plus the travelling, are the real issue – can you say a little more about that?'

● They don't believe there's a solution. Use a question that encourages a sense of possibility, for example, 'You've said you want to sort this – what would "sorted" look like for you?'

● Sometimes, you'll know that they are unlikely to think of anything. Before offering your ideas, you still have options.

    ● Make a gentle observation, without being too directive. For example, 'You've said that it's out of your control and also

> that your boss is rarely around – I'm wondering how those two are linked?'
>
> - Acknowledge the situation. For example, 'Okay, I may have led us up a dark alley, shall we pause a while? What would you like to do?'
>
> Above all, stay relaxed, and easygoing or flexible. An uptight, frustrated coach flounders, while a calm, resourceful coach creates progress. Trust yourself and trust the process!

Stage 5: Completion and close

Just like opening the conversation, this stage is one you're already equipped to deal with, as it's simply a professional close to the discussion. Here, you create a sense of completion and forward momentum. You may need to refer to the original objectives for the session, if there were several of them, just to check that everything's been covered. Your key objectives at this stage are:

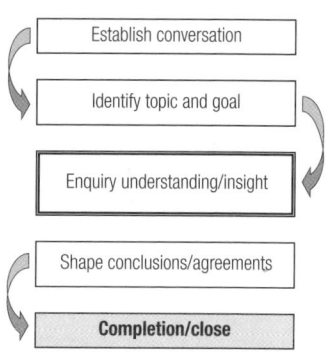

- To confirm that the conversation is complete and that the other person is happy to close
- To indicate that progress has been made
- To create mutual clarity as to what happens now
- To leave your colleague feeling supported as they go forward
- To close the session in a natural way.

Nearly there! Let's see how this conversation might be drawn to a natural close.

Manager	Okay, so you've got your next steps to explore short-term options and tighten the reins on HR.
Tasha	Absolutely.
Manager	Good, I think that's a really firm way forward. Alright, let me just check, is there any support you need from me on this?
Tasha	No, I don't think so. If I come up against anything, I'll ask.
Manager	Great. So has this conversation been useful?
Tasha	Yes, definitely. I think I just needed to think things through.
Manager	Great. I'll be interested to hear how you get on.
Tasha	[laughs] Oh, don't you worry, I'll be telling you. Thanks for your time anyway, that's great.
Manager	Oh, no problem – look we didn't even use the full slot! I'll see you soon.

Here the manager gently rounds off the conversation in a warm and supportive way. I hope you can imagine yourself doing something similar. At no time has the manager had to launch into instruction; they have surfaced the thoughts and views of another person. Of course, it's a convenient scenario as Tasha seemed intelligent and mature for most of the conversation. Here I wanted to show you the basic sequence, rather than exceptions to the sequence. For tackling tougher character types, see the guidance box that follows.

At a glance

What if someone isn't open to being coached?

Occasionally someone may appear confused or less confident in a coaching style of conversation. It may be that you encounter someone who seems less open, or just plain difficult! Remember also that as you learn to behave differently in conversation, that will take time and the issue may be with your approach. To help you decide your best response, check the following scenarios.

1. Where someone is less clear or less confident

Here they may feel uneasy with an increased focus on themselves, their thoughts and their ideas. So, help them relax as you slow down, breathe, (smile!), reduce the pressure and give them time. Summarise the situation as you see it, make an observation or offer a thought. Add your own imperfect musing, for example, 'So I guess I'm thinking . . . ' but hold back on specific ideas or instruction for a while. See also the earlier 'At a glance' toolbox item in this section 'What if someone gets "stuck"?'

2. Where it's your issue, for example because you're new to coaching ideas and behaviours

Here the other person may seem confused by the conversation, perhaps because your approach is different from the usual. As always you have options:

(a) Overt: Tell them what you're attempting/learning to do and ask that they help you to keep the principle of being less directive. Then go back to the basics, for example, 'Okay, so if we operate from a principle that you know enough to figure out the best way forward, and my job is to help you think through the situation – what do we need to talk about here?' Ask them to help you form effective questions (yes, that can work!). Clearly, this option assumes that you are confident in the level of mutual support between you and the other person.

▶

(b) Covert: Go back to basics. Keep a note of simple questions and phrases and pick one or two. For example,

- To keep me clear, can you just summarise the situation for me again? (This also gives you thinking time.)

- Okay, so what's the real issue that we need to solve?

- And what needs to happen going forward?

- What are our options here then?

- If you could change one thing about the situation, what would it be?

For other examples of simple coaching questions, see Chapter 7 – 'Effective questioning'.

(c) Revert: Stop trying to coach and go back to your normal style and approach. Afterwards, reflect on what worked and what didn't. Decide what you're going to do differently next time. Remember, everything is progress and your intention to learn greater flexibility and skill is all you need right now.

3. Where someone is being difficult or less open

Perhaps they give you overly short answers or appear reluctant to respond helpfully to questions. Again, you have options:

(a) Stay calm and continue: Act as if they aren't being difficult (sometimes they'll simply relax and let go of their own resistance). See option 1 for a way to do that.

(b) Point at the behaviour: By this I mean make a gentle observation of what you're doing and how you're experiencing their response. For example, [soft tone] 'Okay, so what I'm trying to do is understand your thoughts about this situation as I'm guessing you have some value to add here. Now from your responses, it seems you don't feel comfortable doing that. How fair is that as an observation perhaps?' From their reply, you can decide to continue seeking to understand their reaction (and support them to relax and talk more freely) or go to option c below.

(c) Decide not to deal with it right now: Switch back to a more directive style and approach (as in option 2c above). Remember that you don't have to stay in a directive style and can flex back to a less directive style at any point. For example, making observations and giving summaries might work later in the conversation. See also Chapter 8 ('A flexible style of influence') for ideas.

 ## In a nutshell

Where the individual has something to discuss

The structure of the Coaching Path is ideal for a pre-scheduled conversation with a colleague, such as a general catch-up or 1:1 update meeting. Our three key stages of the Path, that is identifying the topic and goal, enquiry (create understanding and insight), plus shaping actions and agreements, provide many benefits. For example, the structure naturally places emphasis on **what the person being coached thinks,** and so it helps you, the manager, to maintain a coaching posture. Because clarity of objectives and outcomes is established upfront, and also that mutual understanding (at enquiry stage) is encouraged, an effective workplace conversation happens more easily. When we create the intention of a constructive, solution-focused outcome, this is more likely, for example via a mutually clear, agreed way forward.

CHAPTER 11

Planned conversations: When the manager has the topic or agenda

n our next scenario, we're going to use the same conversation structure (The Coaching Path) to guide us. Let's imagine you want to speak to someone who works for you about some aspect of their work. Maybe you've become concerned about something and want to understand what's happening. Perhaps you've heard something isn't going well, or you've just got out of touch with a situation. So, you arrange to see someone, in a planned conversation. The structure of The Coaching Path would certainly help you coach that conversation. However, we're going to make this one slightly more challenging. We're going to assume that there's an issue with someone's behaviour and you've decided to speak to them about it. The following example shows you how to give negative feedback in a less directive, coaching style.

The Genesis project – setting the scene

You are the project manager of a project called Genesis. The project is to help the whole organisation communicate with each other more effectively. Members of the project team have been gathered from different parts of the company, for example, Sales, Marketing and Finance. Your job is to keep the project team focused on the goals and plans of the project and support them to deliver. Yesterday you attended a meeting where the team got together to give updates on progress and talk through issues. You were surprised that some people appeared irritated with each other, and it affected the atmosphere around the table. Two people seemed to withdraw from participating and simply sat quietly. In particular, you felt that Nico did little to help with his manner and approach. His attitude to other team members seemed curt and even slightly hostile at times, and some of the language he used was emotive, for example, 'That's nonsense'. You have decided that giving Nico some feedback about what you saw might help.

Your objectives for the conversation are:

● To describe what you saw, that is his behavioural responses and the impact they had

● To understand more about what's going on

● To agree a way forward that improves the situation, for example, influence Nico's future behaviour to be more constructive.

Let's remind ourselves of our map for our journey through the conversation: The Coaching Path, as shown again in Figure 11.1.

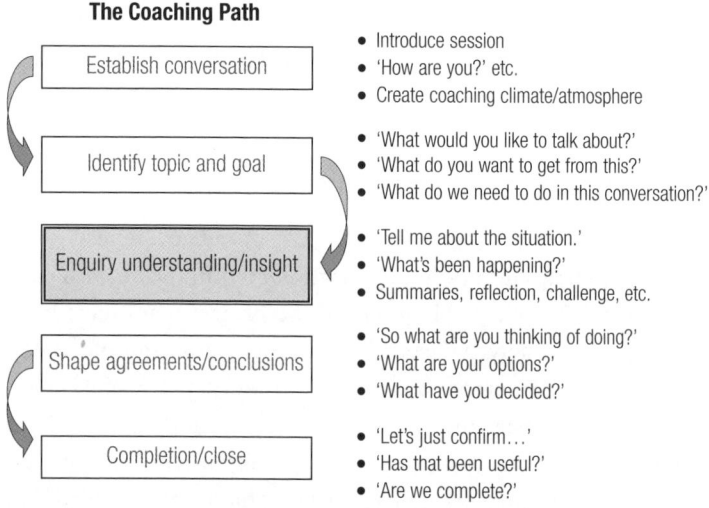

Figure 11.1 The Coaching Path

Much of the conversation flows in a similar way to the previous scenario, with the following exceptions.

- The topic and goal are given by the manager, that is to discuss yesterday's meeting and their observations on behaviour.
- The manager will be prepared to keep offering their views or feedback.
- The manager may have some specific requests to make, which contribute to the 'conclusions and agreements' stage.

Practical preparation

As the manager, you are going to tackle what may be a difficult conversation, so preparing messages and behavioural examples is important. Your other preparation includes setting your intention for your approach to Nico, for example having an open and supportive attitude (rather than being critical or judgmental). For a fuller checklist of personal preparation, see Chapter 9 – 'How to give constructive feedback'.

Stage 1: Establish conversation

Once again, this step builds initial rapport and sets the tone for the meeting. It's also where you, as manager, create a sense of relaxed leadership in the conversation, that is believing 'I can facilitate us through this conversation (I know what I'm doing)'. In our new scenario, let's see how that might sound.

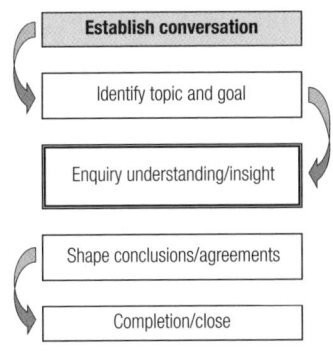

Manager	Hi Nico, thanks for doing this at short notice. Are you okay for time?
Nico	Yes, kind of – I've got another meeting in an hour, but I'm not running that one or anything.
Manager	Well, I hope not to make you late for that. An hour seems plenty of time – let's see how we go, shall we?
Nico	Yes sure, fire away.

Notice how the manager is voicing support for Nico in a respectful way: 'I hope not to make you late for that.' Nico may know that something's not quite right and may be unconsciously preparing himself: 'Yes sure, fire away.' By responding to someone's initial defensiveness or tension with calmness, you encourage their tension to ease or disappear. The manager keeps a relaxed tone and does not react to any tension Nico may be displaying.

The manager is also careful to put their own feelings about what happened in the meeting to one side. Remember, what the manager saw in the meeting yesterday was Nico acting rudely and mildly aggressively, and the manager may have been annoyed by that. But to display any annoyance might:

● Cause the manager to think less clearly

● Portray a judgmental or superior attitude; remember, we want an 'adult-to-adult' conversation, not a 'parent-to-child' tone here

● Place Nico on the defensive, when he realises he's being criticised.

Ironically, for our manager to display irritation would also mirror the very behaviour that provoked this conversation – a curt manner and mild hostility. If we want to encourage maturity in others, we must first begin with ourselves. Watch how the manager maintains an objective view and supportive tone with Nico.

To confirm an earlier idea, our opinions and judgements can colour both our view of someone and the way we respond to them. When we believe someone is 'wrong' – for example in how they act – we often communicate that, either subtly or overtly. This reduces rapport and therefore feelings of trust, openness and mutual support. Once those features of a relationship are reduced so, too, is our ability to influence. So, try to maintain an objective view, if only to give yourself a well-rounded view of a situation.

 Pause and reflect

Test your mood

Use the following to consider how your judgements affect your ability to remain relaxed and objective with someone.

Think about someone in a work situation who has done something you didn't like. Perhaps they displayed a behaviour towards you or others that was difficult for you to handle. Or perhaps they behaved in a way you felt was unfair, unreasonable or just plain nasty. Use a significant example if possible - one that creates discomfort. Now ask yourself the following questions.

Ⓠ How do your feelings towards this person affect your behaviour and attitude towards them?

Ⓠ How are you different with them? For example, what thoughts do you have about them and how does that influence what you do or say, or even how you say it?

Ⓠ If you had to give feedback to that person about this issue - for example what they did that causes you to feel like this - how relaxed and objective could you be?

▶

Now think about what thoughts or feelings you would have to let go of, to remain objective and relaxed with them. For example, try 'giving up' your righteousness about the situation – the idea that you are right, and they are wrong. No matter how illogical that seems, just try it. Or adopt a neutral position of 'I don't know everything about this' or 'There's more to this than I understand'. Or try 'Okay, I'll ignore my feelings of right and wrong just for this exercise' (you can retrieve them later). From that more neutral, objective position, consider:

Q If you assume that they have been doing the best they know (because most of us do), then think again about their actions. How does that enlarge your view of things?

Q Let's assume you're able to be generous towards this person. If your main objective for giving them feedback included trying to understand things from *their* perspective, how would that conversation go?

Q If you were to have this type of conversation, what might be the benefits?

Q How do you feel about this person and situation now?

Let's continue to the next stage on the path.

Stage 2: Identify a clear topic and goal

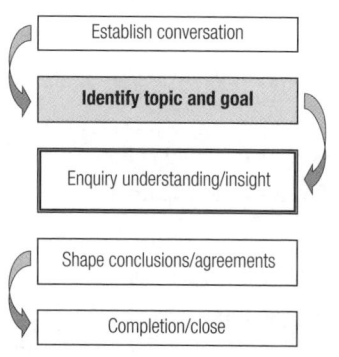

Here the path takes a slightly different turn from the one it took in the previous scenario.

Now the manager simply needs to give the topic in clear, objective terms. For example:

Manager	So, I wanted to talk about the meeting yesterday – I guess it didn't go as well as I'd hoped, and I wanted to talk to you a little about that.
Nico	Right . . .
Manager	I noticed that you didn't appear to be very buoyant in the meeting and I think that probably affected the tone of the meeting a little.
Nico	I'm not sure what you mean. I mean, there were a couple of times when things that were being said bugged me, but then some of what was being said was just garbage.

The manager has begun with a gentle observation – 'You didn't appear to be very buoyant' – rather than an overly specific one, such as 'I noticed you were rude to Sophia on at least four occasions'. That's because the manager is pacing a little, to orientate Nico to the topic, before giving the specifics. The manager has come prepared with some specifics (behavioural observations) and will offer them when it's required. Nico is already preparing his defence, for example, to criticise others, but it's a defence our manager will not engage with.

At a glance

When *you* have the topic, don't try to coach it from them!

In a conversation where you are clear about what you want to discuss, it's pointless trying to obtain your topic from the other person. This is a common pitfall of managers learning to coach and one that normally leads to a dead end. Because we might want to avoid being directive, we forget that it's okay to own the topic of a conversation and have objectives for that conversation. So instead of being willing to state or explain the topic and give objective

▶

feedback, we use a non-directive style in order to 'coach' it out, which may sound like:

Manager	So, I was wondering how you thought the meeting went yesterday?
Nico	I thought it went fine.
Manager	How much of an atmosphere do you think there was in the room?
Nico	I'm not sure. I suppose I hadn't really thought about it.

Clearly, the manager is hoping that Nico will introduce the topic for them and perhaps even 'admit' that there was an issue. It's a flawed strategy and one that works on rare occasions. The manager should wait until the next stage (surface understanding and insight) before adopting a less directive, coaching style of enquiry.

Here's how the manager continues.

Manager	All right, can I say a little more about what I noticed?
Nico	Sure, go ahead.
Manager	I noticed that when Sophia and Erica were giving their updates you seemed to show signs of frustration, like rolling your eyes a bit or sighing, and at one point you told Sophia and Erica their idea was 'nonsense'.
Nico	Well, it is! Anyone knows that staff aren't going to be engaged by yet another poster campaign – we're just sick of them.
Manager	All righ . . . let me say what I saw after that. You see, Sophia seemed to withdraw from the conversation, certainly, she stopped talking, and Erica seemed to do the same – I think she didn't make eye contact with anyone after that.
Nico	Well, isn't that their issue?

Again, the manager is retaining a balanced, relaxed view, despite the signs that Nico is ready to argue. The manager is more focused on their objectives for this 'topic and goal' stage, namely:

- To offer the topic for discussion (complete)
- To give objective feedback based on observation (ongoing)
- To declare their objective for the conversation (ongoing, i.e. implied).

If at any time the manager allows themselves to be 'hooked' (or distracted) by comments that are less relevant to the above points, then the conversation may be side-tracked and lose direction.

Let's see how the manager continues.

Manager	I guess I can see why you'd say that, but for me, it feels like all of our issue. Nico, in yesterday's meeting you didn't appear relaxed and constructive, not how I've seen you being previously. Plus, I thought yesterday was a generally more subdued meeting and I think your responses towards Sophia and Erica might have influenced that.
Nico	Right.
Manager	So, I wanted to talk this through and find out what your view of this is because I want to understand more. I also want to find a way of improving the situation if that's possible.
Nico	Okay, fine.

The manager gives straight, open, direct messages in terms with which Nico is unlikely to disagree. He's unlikely to disagree both because of the previous conversation that's led up to this, and because the manager is 'owning' the comments from a personal perspective, for example using phrases like 'I thought' or 'For me it feels like'. The manager is also staying as neutral as possible, so not saying things like 'You did this and that's really bad' or using emotive words like 'rude' or 'arrogant'. Notice also that there are no clear 'positives' to balance the negatives. There could be some later if they are true, relevant and appropriate. But they are not appropriate now, as they may confuse or reduce the important message.

What's less easy to illustrate here is that the manager must pace the conversation in a way that enables Nico to hear what's being said and process the information logically and emotionally. For example, if the manager rushed through the above observations, without the appropriate pauses, there's a danger that Nico may begin to resist the flow of the conversation because he is struggling to react to what he's just heard. It's important that the manager stays tuned to Nico, rather than dashing through some pre-prepared statements.

So, the manager now has their topic on the table and a declared goal of 'understanding more and improving the situation'. Let's continue down The Coaching Path, picking up all our coaching tools as we go.

Stage 3: Enquiry, understanding and insight

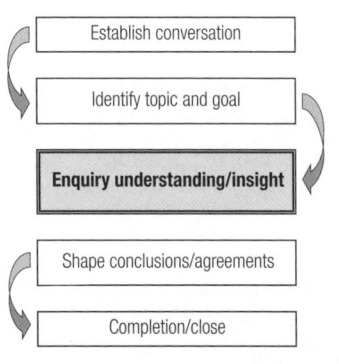

This stage now begins to match the previous chapter's scenario (with Tasha). As the manager, you are using all your skills of rapport, listening, effective questioning and feedback or observation. You want to hear more about the situation from Nico's perspective and know that he's more likely to be open if he feels you are not judging him. You will be in simple 'enquiry' mode for much of the time. Let's continue.

Manager	So, help me understand then – how do you see the situation?
Nico	Well, it's all a mess, isn't it?
Manager	Can you say a bit more about that?
Nico	Yes. We're trying to get Marketing to engage in meaningful communication activities, like the senior management question time, and all they want to do is put up posters.
Manager	Okay, what else?
Nico	I just think that Sophia and Erica are out of their depth – they don't want to tackle the thorny issues, but just the ones that are easy to deal with.
Manager	What are the thorny issues, do you think?
Nico	Well, like the fact that staff still need a clearer appreciation of the new structure and how it all fits together. Putting it up on posters is fine, but people need things explaining. We need dialogue with people – people have got questions.
Manager	So, what should we be doing?
Nico	We need more of an aligned set of activities and tasks – right now everyone's just working from their department's perspective. Marketing knows what they want, Finance has a different agenda – it's just not a coherent plan.

Here the manager is gathering facts, not judging Nico's statements as good or bad, but simply letting him speak. You'll notice that Nico is gradually becoming more objective himself, as he is given space to 'get things off his chest' and perhaps clear some of his frustration. By not reacting to his frustration, the manager does not fuel it, and so gradually Nico's frustration reduces. Once Nico is calmer, he can think more objectively. If we still think Nico needs to say how he's feeling to 'let it go', we might ask him about it, to acknowledge it or help him deal with it. For example:

Manager	Can I ask how you're feeling about all this?
Nico	Yes, really frustrated. Hacked off to be honest. I thought this project was going to make a difference, but now I'm not sure it will.
Manager	So how is how you're feeling affecting your behaviour and performance right now?
Nico	Well, I'm not sure. I mean, I hadn't thought about it.
Manager	Okay, well, look at yesterday's meeting – how did it affect you yesterday?
Nico	Hmmph, that's obvious, isn't it? I guess I'm just irritable about the whole thing.

By acknowledging what Nico is feeling and having him consider how it's affecting him, we are tackling what may be a key issue of Nico's personal development. You may be reading this thinking, 'Yes great, but this is taking too long – why are we asking this guy what he thinks? Just tell him to improve his attitude.' Of course, we could just tell him that he's got a bad attitude and he needs to improve it. It may result in his not being rude in meetings (at least for a while). But his self-awareness may remain the same, for example, he'll still think the rest of the world is wrong and he's right. If we tell Nico to change his attitude, we've achieved compliance but no personal growth. Remember, we're coaching the *person* as much as the issue.

At a glance

A quick summary can work wonders

Part-way through a coaching conversation, a brief, accurate summary from the coach can often work well. By giving a quick summary – either of the whole conversation or just a few key things you've heard – both of you benefit. Remember, a well-timed accurate summary creates clarity, diffuses tension, and gives people additional time to think. A summary can also refocus the discussion or keep it on track if the conversation has digressed. My caution is that using summaries too often can slow a conversation down, or make it feel boring – so it's a great trick when used sparingly!

Let's continue.

Manager	Okay, so let's look at what we've got so far. You're frustrated because the project isn't pulling together and working well together as a team.
Nico	Right.
Manager	And your frustration is causing you to act negatively towards some of the team, which is what we saw yesterday.
Nico	Yes, I guess so. Well, yes, maybe I was a bit snappy.
Manager	And yet you still seem really passionate about what the project is trying to do, because you see it's really needed.
Nico	I do, yes. I really do. You see, even this conversation is annoying because now I'm seeing that the very thing I'm saying we should be doing is what I'm not doing – which is working as a team.

By a simple, relaxed summary, the manager takes the pressure off Nico and allows him to reflect on what he's been saying. Again, the space and the ability to detach a little have helped Nico realise something else, namely that he's part of the problem rather than part of the solution. It's probably worth digging one last time into Nico's thoughts, just to see what's there.

Manager	All right, so can I ask you, what thoughts are you having now about all this?
Nico	Well, to be honest, I think I need to refocus a little. I've obviously let things get to me and it's not helping.
Manager	I'd probably agree with that. So, what do you need to do?
Nico	I think I need to work out what my main frustrations are and work on those. I don't think it's everything or everyone; I think it's just some key issues that I think aren't being dealt with.

Now, in real life we may want to continue this part of the discussion, to help surface more of Nico's ideas. We'd probably help him work out what his main frustrations are and what he thinks are the key issues that need to be dealt with.

Using simple, open questions the manager can help Nico to reflect in a useful way, for example:

● Okay, so what needs to happen?

● What's important here, do you think?

● What else seems relevant to think about?

I'll add that the manager needs to be ready to give further feedback or opinion, for example, 'I'm not sure that's enough'. But for the purposes of demonstration, let's move on to the next stage.

At a glance

Don't push too hard on actions – it may cost you equality

Sometimes we spoil the 'adult-to-adult' sense of a coaching conversation right at the end, by being pedantic or forceful when agreeing on actions. For example, after coaching someone really well to create ideas around a situation, we suddenly become dominant by saying something like 'Right, so what are you going to do and by when – what am I going to see from this?'

Remember:

- Different people and situations need different levels of agreement or detail.
- You need to let go of the 'I'm in charge' attitude in favour of 'I know I can trust you'.

Most things can be a 'longer game'. For example, if I say I'll do something and then do not do it, you can pick that up at our next meeting. If over time this becomes a pattern of behaviour, you can tackle the pattern of behaviour directly, for example 'I notice that some of the actions you're committing to aren't getting done. Can we talk about that?'

Remember, you have an ongoing relationship with the people who work with you, and you encourage maturity when you demonstrate it yourself.

Stage 4: Shape conclusions and agreements

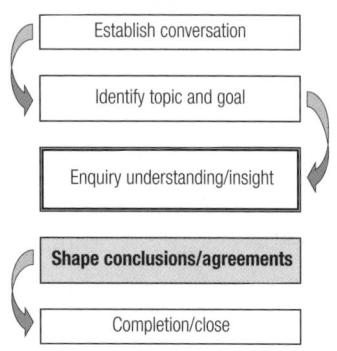

Establish conversation

Identify topic and goal

Enquiry understanding/insight

Shape conclusions/agreements

Completion/close

In this stage, we pull together the main threads of the conversation and see what we've got: the conclusions, ideas and a way forward. In real conversations, ideas or solutions often surface in the previous stage and then get refined in this stage. In our abridged example with Nico, this hasn't yet happened, although certainly, he seems ready to think about ideas now; let's continue.

Manager	Okay, so you feel that you've got some key issues that you feel strongly about, such as the team not pulling together, so not focusing on the main communications issues that the project is set up to address.
Nico	Yes, and it's probably just a few key things. If we sorted those, we'd do a lot of good.
Manager	I agree, and with your links into the business, you're probably in a good position to see what those really are. So, what are you thinking of doing?

That final question ('So, what are you thinking of doing?') is quite significant, in that the manager has judged that Nico is ready to move away from discussing problems and conclusions and instead move towards a solution. The question also assumes that Nico *can* decide, which is a clear demonstration of the manager's trust in Nico's ability. That encourages a sense of empowerment in Nico. Of course, if Nico gives an idea that is either inappropriate or just plain crazy, then the manager can intervene. For example, when hearing an ill-considered plan, the manager may ask a question that causes Nico to look at the impact of the action, for example, 'How will Marketing react to that, do you think?' Or if the idea is really crazy, the manager can offer a gentle opinion, for example 'I think that might be outside the original terms we've agreed for the project'. We can still influence without being parental or controlling – we don't have to say, 'You can't do that, you're not allowed to'.

Let's continue after the 'So, what are you thinking of doing?' question.

Nico	I think I'd like to call the team together again and tell them my frustrations. To be fair, I think many of us are feeling the same way – I know Dave definitely is. Of course, I could go in and suggest a plan forwards, but it would be better if we did that together.
Manager	I think that's wise – let people stay involved. Okay, what do you see as the shape of that session?
Nico	I think we need more of an open discussion about how it felt when we first started the project and how it is feeling now. Then we need to decide on refocusing a little.
Manager	Okay, and I guess I'm still wondering, what's going to stop that being a session that goes the same way as yesterday?
Nico	Yes, well, that's down to me a bit, isn't it? I probably need to build some bridges with some people, and I need to think about that. Maybe it's something that would be better done informally – I'm not sure.
Manager	I think people would welcome that and I do think it would create a better feel for the next meeting. So, what's the way forward?

Nico	Right, yes, I think I need to go away and plan that session. I need to come up with an outline or something – nothing fancy – I just can't get to it now.
Manager	Yes, I can see that – it's probably worth taking a little time over. So, when will I hear from you again?
Nico	Give me until tomorrow – I want to speak to a couple of people.

As you can see, the manager is doing very little here. To demonstrate the less directive posture, I've deliberately reduced the amount of input from the manager. In reality, the manager might reasonably offer more views or observations, for example, that:

● Nico's frustrations are impairing his ability to stay resourceful and play a valuable role within the team.

● Nico can sometimes get 'stuck' in the problem rather than focus on solutions.

● Nico is a lot more powerful when he helps people, like Sophia, to succeed rather than withdrawing support from them.

Again, these are all developmental points intended to support Nico, rather than instructions aimed at 'fixing' the issues. Any or all of these might comfortably sit within the 'enquiry and understanding' stage, or possibly 'shape conclusions and agreements'. But any earlier and they may feel a little too judgemental (and create a defensive response). What's important is that they are communicated in such a way that Nico feels his manager is trying to support him to be successful, rather than being critical, for example 'having a go'.

Okay, we are nearly there, let's wrap this up.

Stage 5: Completion and close

Here we are just drawing the conversation to a close while leaving the 'door open' to pick the conversation up again if we need to. Again, you've got lots of experience at ending conversations in an appropriately warm way, so here's how this one ends.

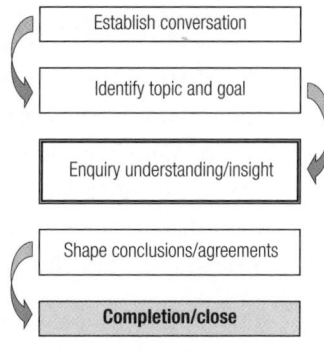

Manager	Okay, that sounds like a plan. So, can I ask, are we done here? Has that been useful?
Nico	Yes, it has, it's a bit of a relief really. Yes, I feel a bit better about the whole thing now.
Manager	All right, Nico, well thanks for that. I'll see you later then. Have a good day.

Now you may be wondering, 'Okay, so where's the admission of guilt? When is Nico going to apologise to Sophia and Erica? Is that it?' Well, here's what we need to remember.

- We are dealing with adults in an adult situation (not school, where people get punished). Our objective was not to prove Nico wrong or to make him suffer.

- We trust Nico is a mature adult with basically good intentions: he's voiced that he needs to 'build some bridges' and we can probably assume that means with Sophia and Erica. We've had enough of a conversation about his behaviour to make it clear that it has negative consequences.

- While we have a duty of care for Sophia and Erica, ultimately, they are responsible for themselves, and to 'rescue' them too much may reduce or demean their position.

The importance of effective follow-up

Nico has said that he'll come back in a couple of days with an update and that presents an opportunity for a follow-up conversation of some sort, either to enquire about or acknowledge progress. You also want to sustain your positive intention and support for Nico as he works to improve his awareness and behaviour in this situation and similar situations in future.

The topic is also relevant to Nico's ongoing professional development and so you may choose to refer to the idea again, perhaps as part of a regular update meeting. Obviously, if the problem behaviour continues, then you may pick up the conversation sooner. Remember, managing people is a longer game, and real change often takes a little longer to develop.

In a nutshell

In your role as a manager who is focused on the performance of others, The Coaching Path helps you to have constructive conversations relating to negative tendencies or behaviour. Unlike the previous scenario, where the person you are coaching is encouraged to 'own' the conversation throughout, in this example, you as the manager retain the upfront 'topic and goal'. When you are clear that you own the topic and goal for the conversation, you retain control of that, as is appropriate. You then use the 'enquiry' stage to engage the other person and understand their view of the situation. Once again, at the stage of 'shape agreements', we encourage a constructive way forward, for example 'here's what will be different in future'.

CHAPTER 12

Planned
conversation:
Both the
individual and
the manager
have topics to
discuss

This final planned scenario builds on the previous two by presenting a situation where both the manager and the subordinate have things they want to discuss. For completeness, we'll start at the beginning and demonstrate the opening of the conversation. But in this scenario, your challenge is mostly about deciding what's 'coachable' (what can be handled in a less directive style) and what's not (where you simply need to confirm or give information). My challenge is to show you how actually most things are coachable and that when you withhold your natural inclination to 'tell' you'll discover this for yourself.

This time we'll imagine that you're with one of your team for a regular update meeting. They know they need to come prepared with their objectives, and they normally bring a list of these. There are also topics you'd like to discuss, so you want to add them to the list. The meeting is with Marla, who runs a small team in a busy call centre.

Stage 1: Establish the conversation

Here's the initial stage where you say hello, get comfortable and create a sense of a work-related conversation. As before, you're in the best position to judge how formal or informal you need to be

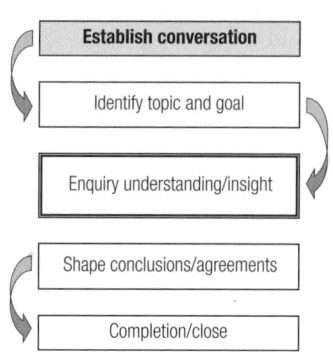

but try to keep all these types of conversations as relaxed as possible. Too much 'professional speak' can create a lack of equality in the conversation and reduce rapport (and so openness).

Manager	Marla, hi. Gosh, it's a bit cold in here, let me just adjust the thermostat. How are you, how are things?
Marla	Well, great really. Well, busy, as you know, I haven't really got time for this, but it seems ages since I saw you.
Manager	I know, it'll be Christmas next! Right, well, let's get going – how long have we got for this, is it 45 minutes?
Marla	Yes, but if this room doesn't warm up, I'll be out sooner than that!

As you can see, lots of familiarity and rapport. Obviously, if you don't know someone well you might be a little more formal, but you are in the best position to judge what's appropriate for each individual.

At a glance

Stop playing fix-it!

Coaching conversations are a challenge for managers, as they often must listen to a problem which affects them in some way. For example, when your team member declares they can't cope with their workload, you feel ultimately accountable for that. So, most managers want to 'fix' the issue quickly, for example by telling subordinates what to do, or by taking action in some way. To coach effectively, it's crucial that we go into coaching mode here, rather than 'hear problem – fix problem' mode. For you, as a manager, it may feel as though you must stay quiet or 'sit on your hands' in the conversation. It demands both self-awareness, that is you need to realise you've gone into 'fix-it' mode, and also self-management. Over time, the whole process becomes more natural, especially once you see the benefits for yourself.

Stage 2: Identify a clear topic and goal

Here we'll build the topic together, as both the manager and Marla have things they want to discuss. It's best to hear from Marla first, as she's the person responsible for her situation. We also want to keep a sense that she needs to own getting the most out of the session and needs to come ready to work in the conversation. Let's continue the discussion.

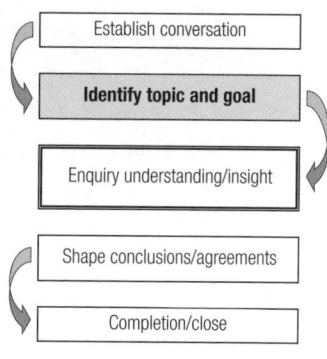

Establish conversation

Identify topic and goal

Enquiry understanding/insight

Shape conclusions/agreements

Completion/close

Manager	All right, so let's just focus this a little then. Tell me, what would you like to get from this conversation?
Marla	Well, I want to talk about three things: the latest results of our fabulous push on sales – we've just heard how we've done so far with that, plus, the current budget allocation – I've had some ideas about that. Oh, and I also want to get your input on a bit of a behaviour issue I've got with someone in my team.
Manager	Great, and I'd like to pick up with you from last time about the challenges we were having with escalated customer complaints and related social media reviews.
Marla	Ah yes, I've got some news on that too.

Definition

Sympathy

The act of sharing feelings with another person. For example, if you're upset, I'll get upset too, or if you're sad, so am I.

Empathy

The ability to relate to, appreciate or understand the feelings of someone else, without necessarily taking on that emotion ourselves.

In coaching, empathy is normally more appropriate than sympathy. For example, 'I can appreciate that this is upsetting' is more appropriate than this expression of sympathy: 'That's awful, it's making me angry too.'

In the first empathetic statement, we remain objective and impartial, whereas, in the sympathetic example, we also become angry and so less objective. You want to support the individual to stay resourceful in the conversation and helping them stay angry might not help. Occasionally, however, empathy may appear cold, and sympathy is more appropriate, for example in genuinely upsetting events such as crisis, loss or trauma.

What's coachable and what's not?

Now, from Marla's and the manager's lists of topics they'd like to cover, I hope you'll notice that some of the topics seem more 'coachable' than others.

- **The sales results:** These are probably good news that Marla wants to share. Assuming that there isn't an issue with them, that is they're actually pretty good, then that's probably not a topic that will be helped by the Coaching Path. However, you might want to ask a few coaching questions to foster learning, such as 'So how can we build on these results going forward?'

- **The budget allocation:** Marla appears to have ideas to change or improve this in some way. So, this may involve you giving support or instead clarifying what's possible. Perhaps you're supporting her ideas or else you are explaining what Marla needs to do according to the process. This may be an occasion where a directive style is more appropriate, for example, 'Yes, you're right, that's what we need' or 'No, we can't do that', and so on. Or it might indeed be coachable, and Marla simply needs a little time and space to work out her own answers for herself. Perhaps she's wondering how much is assigned in the budget for training this year and is hesitant about that. By facilitating her thought processes (using coaching behaviours), you can help her.

- **The issue with a member of her team:** This appears the most obviously suited for the Coaching Path. After all, Marla is managing the individual and her ability to cope with them is key to her role. If she's got an issue with someone, the best value you can add is probably to help her decide how to tackle it.

- **The customer complaints issues:** This is also probably a coaching opportunity. It's implied that this is an issue that Marla has already discussed, and the manager wants an update. By using coaching tools such as enquiry and powerful questions, the manager can support Marla to stay resourceful around that situation.

Let's move the conversation along this stage of the path: Identify clear topic(s) and goal.

Manager	Right, well, I make that four things.
Marla	Yes: the results, the budget, the issue with Phoebe and the customer complaints. I'll also add that those last two are sort of linked.
Manager	Okay, so where would you like to start?

Marla	The Phoebe thing I guess – it's nagging me a bit. Can we do that first?
Manager	Yes, let's start with that then. Just so that I'm clear, what do you want to get out of talking this through?
Marla	Well, I think I should probably sack her, but I want to know if I'm doing the right thing.

So here we have Marla's topic, the objective and the goal for the conversation. It's a perfect topic to adopt a less directive posture on, as it's all about Marla's ability to deal with a difficult member of her team. There's a temptation for the manager to become involved in what might be a 'juicy issue' and give advice in a potentially dramatic situation. But as a manager, it's easier to coach when you stay objective and impartial. After Marla's last statement, the manager might easily choose to move on to the next stage, 'enquiry and understanding'. So, let's do that.

> It's easier to coach when you stay objective and impartial

Stage 3: Enquiry, understanding and insight

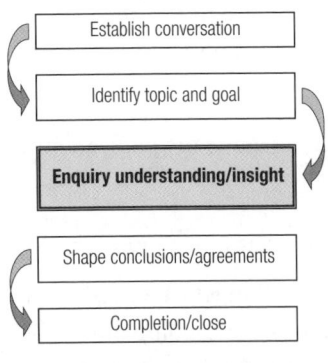

So here we move into enquiry mode around the situation with Phoebe. Remember that we're seeking to understand – surfacing Marla's thoughts, ideas and views – rather than trying to arrive at a smart solution to the situation. As always, we're assuming the answers will come from Marla.

Manager	Okay, can you tell me a little more about the situation with Phoebe then?

Marla	Well, on Friday things came to a head. I overheard Phoebe being really rude to a customer on the telephone and had to take her to one side and talk to her about it.
Manager	Okay.
Marla	And her attitude was the same as I'd experienced previously – she seems to lose her temper at the slightest thing and then regret it later. She knew immediately that what she'd said to the customer was inappropriate, but once again in the heat of the moment, she'd been defensive and argumentative.
Manager	And you've had these discussions before, haven't you?
Marla	Oh yes, several times – at least five, I'd say. That's what makes me think I should really consider letting her go. I suppose it's not fair on the rest of the team really.
Manager	You seem a bit reluctant about that.

Here the manager is adopting a more detached perspective – which is one of the benefits of not trying to 'fix' the issue or give any advice. Because the manager is more detached, they can empathise, or relate to Marla's apparent 'mood'. By reflecting this back to Marla, it creates a worthwhile shift in the conversation.

At a glance

Coaching isn't just asking questions

When we learn to coach, we often assume that the principle 'Don't tell people what to do' means 'Make people think by asking questions'. This means that we think that a coaching conversation is

▶

> a series of questions and very little else. That's not true! Asking
> someone a list of questions can place them (and you) under
> pressure, so remember to do all the other conversational 'stuff' like
> summarising, confirming, musing or 'waffle' – for example 'Right,
> got it, that's quite a large piece of work then, isn't it?' or 'Right . . .
> okay . . . oh . . . ' Take the pressure off and let it feel natural –
> remember, coaching is always a conversation. The behaviours
> outlined in Chapter 8 – 'Develop a flexible style of influence' –
> will enable your coaching conversations to flow naturally.

To continue the conversation:

Marla	Well, to be fair, I am. I mean she's a nice girl, a lovely girl really, she can just be a bit immature, if you know what I mean. She just needs to calm down a bit, you know, realise it's not school and it's not a teacher that's telling her off – it's a customer who often has a genuine cause for complaint.
Manager	So, what causes her to lose her temper, do you think?
Marla	[pauses] You know, I think it's that she takes things personally. It's like it's her against the customer or even the world! It's not like she's even the one that's at fault, it's the service engineers who have often made the mistake. But you'd think to admit we've made a mistake would kill her.
Manager	So, what are you thinking of doing?
Marla	Well, on Friday I honestly felt like 'enough is enough', and that I needed to accept that things just aren't going to change.
Manager	And now?

Again, the manager is able to notice what isn't being said, because of their objective view of the conversation, that is that Marla is in two minds about the situation. The manager's role is to help her decide what she wants to do.

Marla	Oh, I don't know – take her by the scruff of the neck probably! She's such a feisty character. I just feel she's got real potential, you know – she's got more about her than most people her age. Maybe she just needs some training or something.
Manager	So, what are you considering?

That last question is what I'd call 'artfully vague', in that it leaves the potential response very broad while moving the conversation on a little by gently probing for potential ideas.

Marla	I'm not sure. I think she'd benefit from hearing how she's supposed to handle difficult customers. She could do with taking a leaf out of Neil's book – he'd make a good peacekeeper for the UN that one, so cool in a crisis.
Manager	And is that possible?
Marla	You know, it probably is. I mean, we could soon hook her up to the call recording equipment and she could listen to some of Neil's calls on playback.

Again, our manager is doing very little except to facilitate Marla's thoughts and allow her to express her thoughts and feelings. The benefit is that Marla appears to be getting clearer in her own mind and making her own decisions. We're now ready to go to the next stage, 'shape conclusions and agreements'.

Stage 4: Shape conclusions and agreements

In this stage, we pull the conversation together, so Marla can decide what she's got from the conversation and be clear about what she's decided to do going forwards.

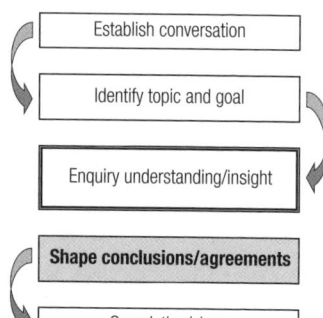

Manager	All right, so what have you decided in this conversation?
Marla	[laughs] Well, I'm obviously not going to sack her, am I? I think she's my own personal challenge I won't let go of!
Manager	[laughs] Yes, I do think it sounds like she's worth trying something different with. What are you going to do?
Marla	I'm going to get her to sit next to Neil, and I'm also going to get her to listen to some of his calls. And if that doesn't work, I'm going to run out screaming or something!
Manager	[laughs] Okay, so if that happens, I'll know who's to blame! I do think it's a good plan though, it's wonderful to think you might turn this around – let me know how you get on; I'll be interested to hear.

Marla has benefited from getting the problem off her chest and from finding out how she really feels, now her initial frustration has been expressed. Marla and the manager had more topics for discussion, so the short dialogue below illustrates how to continue with those.

Manager	Right, okay, let's look at our other topics then, my notes say budget requirements, customer complaints and the push on sales, where would you like to go next?
Marla	Let's do the budget allocation first as there's just one idea there to explore, then the progress we've made with those couple of complaints and then finish on the good news coming out of the recent sales campaigns.
Manager	Sounds great, okay help me understand the situation with the budget then.

Decide when to coach (and when not to coach)

As previously, it's up to you as the manager to decide if it's relevant or appropriate to coach the remaining topics. To do this, you will consider:

1 Is this a topic where Marla needs support to decide something or wants your help to get clearer about that? For example 'A customer is being unfairly critical of us on social media and I'm unsure how we might respond online.'

2 Is this something that Marla simply wants you to be aware of? For example 'this customer complained, we got back to him, explained and settled the matter, he's now very happy' and so on.

3 Is this something that only you can judge/decide/approve? For example 'I want to reallocate some of the surplus recruitment budgets to training instead and I need your sign-off for that.'

From the above, the first scenario seems most coachable, while the second is probably something for you to listen to, and perhaps offer observations, or encouragement. The third scenario seems to prompt you to be directive (say 'yes', 'no' or 'maybe . . . '). However, it's important to remember that when we have developed a flexible style of conversation, (see The Steppingstones Model, from Chapter 8) we can change our style of influence mid-conversation. Using scenario 2 (the complaining customer), the following sample dialogue illustrates this:

Marla	So, we explained to the customer that the mix-up had been caused when he'd entered the same item in a different colour but given us the discount code only once. He realised that it was basically his fault and sort of apologised, he's withdrawn the complaint, deleted his nasty social media post and gone away feeling a little embarrassed, I think.
Manager	That's a nice turnaround, isn't it? Especially given how angry he sounded on our Facebook page! I'm just wondering, what's here for us to learn do you think?
Marla	I'm not sure, what do you mean?
Manager	I'm just wondering how we can avoid this happening again; it seems a simple mistake to make.
Marla	Well, I'm not sure as I don't know if there's any way that the online order form could check or spot that.
Manager	[uses silence]
Marla	Let me have a word with the tech support guys and see if there's some kind of fix available to that. Maybe there's a check they can do or something.

What might have been a simple update point, 'this customer complaint went away,' has been something that Marla has been encouraged to see differently. Of course, the manager could have just said, 'great and see if there's a tech fix for this in future,' but by now we know the downsides of doing that, such as teaching Marla to expect that her manager will think for her.

To maintain our pace, instead of working in detail through the remaining topics, let's assume we're now ready to move to the final stage: 'Completion and close'.

Stage 5: Completion and close

Here we check that it's okay to close the conversation, and then end it in an appropriate way. Given the familiarity between Marla and her manager, this is straightforward.

Establish conversation	
Identify topic and goal	
Enquiry understanding/insight	
Shape conclusions/agreements	
Completion/close	

Manager	Alright, Marla, so let me just check – are we okay to complete this conversation here?
Marla	Yes, that's fine. I'm happy with where we've got to, especially with Phoebe, I'm still smiling at that outcome.
Manager	[chuckles] Right, agreed, and we've covered quite a lot in a fairly short space of time which is great.
Marla	Absolutely, right I've got a customer call back at 3 pm so I'll see you soon, thanks for that.

Please notice that the relaxed and informal style of this conversation is an indication of confident and effective coaching. Again, it's important that you retain your own natural conversational style while adopting simple principles such as listening more, talking less and assuming that someone else can come up with valid insights, conclusions and ideas.

In a nutshell

Where both manager and colleague have topics to discuss

It's both possible and helpful to blend a coaching approach into a conversation where you also choose to be directive, or straight to the point. Clearly, not every situation suits a coaching approach, and the principles here will help you judge that for yourself. Also, a coaching style of conversation can be fatiguing for the person being coached, especially if they are new to that. Through the process of enquiry, they are being challenged to work harder in the conversation, as they are asked to share their thoughts and ideas 'in the moment'.

When we develop a more flexible style of influence, for example using The Steppingstones Model, our use of coaching becomes much more natural and pragmatic to everyday work conversations.

CHAPTER 13

Unplanned conversations: Response Coaching

Response Coaching is when we adopt a coaching posture as a natural response to someone's day-to-day issues or challenges. When someone brings you an issue, rather than fix the problem (or tell them what they should do) you coach them to think and act for themselves. Most opportunities to use Response Coaching happen in the live work environment, for example in everyday discussions and chats with your colleagues. Response Coaching principles work well for Zoom or Teams meetings, telephone calls and even in email communication. Situations might range from a trivial question from a junior colleague, such as 'The meeting room's double-booked, what do we do?', to a more significant 'The system's gone down and we can't process any orders'. As a manager, a coached response needs to create progress as good as, or better than, any directive instruction. So how do we coach 'on the hoof' like this and still make progress on tasks? Figure 13.1 illustrates a three-step model that's designed to help.

Figure 13.1 Response Coaching

Let's imagine that you're managing a team of call operatives who work in a busy call centre. One of the team, Tim, approaches you with a problem he hopes you'll solve for him: 'I've got a customer on the line who wants to return a faulty product, but he's three days out of the 12-month guarantee period – what should I tell him?'

You decide that this is the type of query that Tim should be capable of answering himself. Perhaps you want to encourage his confidence, explore his potential, or simply challenge his typical posture of 'I'll avoid taking responsibility here'.

At a glance

Principles to work from

Here's a quick reminder of our principles that support Response Coaching situations.

- This is an 'adult-to-adult' conversation, that is you are both mature and equal in the conversation.

- The other person is responsible both for the issue they bring and for their actions in relation to that issue – not in a 'blame' sense, but in being empowered to think and act.

- They have their own thoughts about the situation or can be challenged to create a constructive way forward for themselves.

- You add value to the conversation by facilitating their thoughts and ideas, using effective questions, and offering your observations and feedback.

- While you probably have experience and expert advice you could offer, you prefer that they come up with solutions and so you avoid giving answers until it becomes silly not to. Even then, you'll make 'gentle offers', for example, 'Can I offer a thought?'

Stage 1: Seek to understand

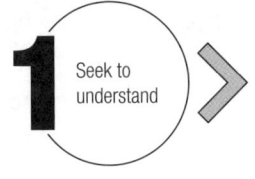

First, begin the process of questioning and listening, so you can reveal the full facts of the situation and areas you might explore, including:

- So, what are the key facts – for example, what happened?
- What seems important in this situation?
- What else seems relevant?

Here is where we build quick clarity of the situation for both the manager and the team member. Let's continue the Tim example. During the following dialogue, Tim is encouraged to 'work' in the conversation, as the manager uses simple questions, summaries, and observations. This begins the conversation in a way that allows Tim to maintain a sense of ownership. It also becomes a way of 'interrupting' a manager's old habits, as the manager focuses on understanding, rather than 'fixing'. As usual, I've simplified the dialogue to reduce your reading time. Here's how the conversation might sound.

Tim	I've got a customer on the line who wants to return a faulty product, but he's three days out of the 12-month guarantee period – what should I tell him?
Manager	Alright, what are the other facts?
Tim	Well, it's a petrol lawnmower – he says he's only used it a few times, he bought it before his garden was actually finished. Anyway, he got it out for the first time this year and the starter cord has snapped.
Manager	So, what is he asking for?

Tim	Well, he thought it was still in the guarantee period, so he was expecting us either to replace it or fix it. I've told him we might not do either – after all, it's out of guarantee.
Manager	Alright, anything else?
Tim	I don't know – what do you mean?
Manager	Well, before we can make a decision, what else do we need to consider?
Tim	Errr, I don't know. Well, I guess the issue of fairness or customer service or something . . . I mean, he's only used it a few times. Plus, he seems like a really straight bloke – he's not trying it on or anything.

The manager is questioning the team member to display the facts of the situation, to both of them. The manager is doing that in a way that helps Tim make a decision for the current issue and also teaches Tim how to think through a similar future issue. Next time Tim has a similar situation, he's likely to repeat a similar process himself, for example saying to himself 'Okay, to make a decision, what do I need to consider?'

Let's continue to the next stage.

At a glance

Coaching is a different type of contribution

When you coach you add value in a different way, that is you facilitate the thought processes of someone else. That can take a little getting used to when you might know the answer to a situation and not offer it. That's because you've decided the benefits of developing people's thought processes for themselves are more valuable to you than a 'fast fix'. That's what we mean by 'teach a hungry man to fish'. Over time, your subordinates learn to expect this process, which teaches them to adopt the same thought process by themselves – and that's empowerment.

Stage 2: Focus on the potential of the other person

This stage requires the manager to shift their typical 'fix-it' mind-set, as they assume that Tim is the source of the solution. As you imagine yourself as a manager here, you must ignore your own compulsion to have the answer. In our scenario, after hearing what Tim has just said, the manager is probably very able to decide what should happen. But instead, they must work to gain conclusions, options and actions from the *subordinate*. For example, the manager can ask:

- So, what options do we/you have?
- Alright, what are you proposing?
- What do you want to do now?

Here our manager facilitates the team member to think and come up with proposals or ideas. Of course, the team member might not be able to think of anything, or what they do suggest may be unreasonable or inappropriate. But remember, the manager has other things they can do first, before giving direct instruction. For example, the manager can:

- Offer a summary, for example 'So he's hardly used it – and you trust him about that – and it's just the starter cord that's broken. You're concerned that we need to offer good service and you need to decide what that is'

- Make an observation, for example 'Well, you seem to think we should do something to help – what's fair, do you think?'

Here's how the dialogue might continue.

Manager	So, what are your options?
Tim	Well, we can do nothing – tell him we can't help. Or we can offer to fix it or even replace it. I guess we could even refund it, but that seems a bit much . . .
Manager	So, what's reasonable?
Tim	I think we should offer to fix it really.

The manager has effectively 'walked through' a logical decision-making process with Tim that has encouraged Tim to form his own conclusion and decision. The manager has influenced Tim's thoughts, without controlling them. For example, by asking 'What's reasonable?' the manager reminds Tim that he needs to keep his suggestion within logical commercial boundaries. This helps Tim balance a 'wonderful' solution with a reasonable one. If we wanted to reduce the manager's influence further, we would have asked a question that was even more open, for example, 'So what do you want to do?'

Stage 3: Encourage action

This stage creates engagement and motivates your team member to act. We make sure that ownership of the solution remains with them, and leaves you, the manager, to offer support as appropriate. For example, the manager might say:

- That sounds like a good plan, what's the next step then?
- Is there any support from me you need with that?
- Great – it'll be good to hear how you get on.

This scenario is straightforward, plus we need to come to a conclusion quickly (the customer is on hold, remember!). Here's a simple close to this example.

Manager	Okay, so what are you going to do?
Tim	I'll tell him we'll fix it and then arrange for a service engineer to call around.
Manager	Great, that sounds like a good solution for him and us – thanks for that.

This is a simple example to demonstrate the three-step Response Coaching model. The model isn't doing anything clever or complex. But it does encourage an important shift in mindset, from fixing to coaching. As a manager, your challenge isn't to understand the model, it's remembering to use it! To coach consistently, you must be self-aware in these circumstances – and recognise when you don't need to give the answer.

But surely fixing the issue is faster?

Here's the same example where the manager chooses to 'fix it' rather than coach the situation.

Tim	I've got a customer on the line who wants to return a faulty product, but he's three days out of the 12-month guarantee period – what should I tell him?
Manager	All right, what are the main facts?
Tim	Well, it's a petrol lawnmower – he says he's only used it a few times, he bought it before his garden was actually finished. Anyway, he got it out for the first time this year and the starter cord has snapped.
Manager	So, what is he asking us for?
Tim	Well, he thought it was still in the guarantee period, so he was expecting us either to replace it or fix it. I've told him we might not do either – after all, it's out of guarantee.
Manager	All right, anything else?
Tim	I don't know – what do you mean?
Manager	Okay, tell him we'll fix it, but actually, we shouldn't be doing that – he is out of the 12-month period after all.
Tim	Okay, boss – will do.

Bish bash bosh (boss) . . . sorted – so where's the issue?

Some people would argue that the above exchange is shorter, and the time pressure justifies simply telling Tim what to do. But remember that while this directive exchange has a time benefit, it also has a time cost, because the next time Tim gets a similar question from a customer, he's likely to come back requiring the same 'Solomon'-like judgement on a situation.

Tim is also likely to feel like his role is pretty low level and he's required to obtain permission for even the most mundane of decisions. Tim might prefer that (for various reasons), or he may be frustrated by it, especially if he considers himself as having some potential, ambition or intelligence.

Where the manager's response is consistently a coaching one, Tim is likely to feel able to work out for himself what he should do *and* that his manager trusts him to decide. This achieves the goal of many organisations – an empowered workforce who think and act responsibly.

> The goal of many organisations – an empowered workforce who think and act responsibly

Learn to coach people by email – it's often easier!

Coaching by email is the perfect place to practise your coaching responses, simply because in the written form you have time to review, reflect and respond from your coaching principles, such as:

- I need to keep ownership of the issue with them.
- I need to encourage them to reply with suggestions, proposals and ideas.
- I'll avoid taking ownership of the situation too quickly.

First, explore how directive you are typically; review some of your recent email exchanges with team members, then ask yourself:

1   How quickly do I give people an answer to their problem, or tell them what to do?

2   How often do I leave a matter with them, and encourage them to decide?

3   How much do I impose my own will/opinion on the situation when actually I don't need to?

Of course, sometimes the situation does not allow you to coach; if that's true then simply tell people what they should do. Your challenge is to find all those other situations where actually, you took quick control of a situation/or rescued it and you didn't need to.

Here are examples of phrases you might use over email.

● 'I'm interested in your thoughts for a potential way forward – what ideas do you have?'

● 'You seem to have good knowledge of the issue here – can you give me some options for a way forward?'

● 'So clearly this is an issue we need to resolve, what do you suggest might work?'

You can also create your own pretty quickly, that is in a style and manner that feels natural for you.

As you practise coaching responses during email exchanges, over time it's likely that your mail inbox will have less in it, as people anticipate your response and get straight to action. Alternatively, the content of people's emails may be less frustrating to you, as people are asking for support only when they really need it.

In a nutshell

Response Coaching

The ability to respond in the live environment using coaching principles demands that we compress all previous ideas, beliefs and skills into an 'in the moment' conversation/exchange. Response Coaching is the name we give to this type of exchange, that is coaching as a natural response to everyday problems and challenges from other people. It's a hugely versatile tool, which can be used in person, over video conference meetings, emails and telephone conversations. Whilst the ideas which underpin our three-step Response Coaching tool are simple, the challenges demand that managers think differently under pressure. For example, when someone has brought you a tricky (or interesting!) problem and wants you to fix it. The manager's challenge is to remember that by focussing on the other person as the source of the solution, it's possible to help create a constructive way forward AND encourage them to learn, develop and grow.

In a nutshell

Application: Make coaching work for you

Coaching principles can be adapted to assist many everyday work situations. This potential ranges from a formal review meeting to discuss someone's performance, to a bite-sized conversation in the canteen, on the telephone, and so on. The Coaching Path and the Response Coaching models are designed to help you in any situation you might encounter. Much of your challenge is to stay self-aware, for example of your own compulsions to help or fix the situation, by giving quick and easy answers. When you (and your colleagues) experience the benefits of your coaching, then coaching becomes a behaviour you'll naturally want to use more often.

PART 4

Action

CHAPTER 14

Take your learning forward

I n this final chapter, we'll consider where you are now in terms of your ability to coach. We'll also focus on your journey ahead, as one that takes you towards coaching being a natural and straightforward thing to do in your work situations. As usual, I'll offer routines for you to work through, to help equip you for your travels. I will also be asking you some questions, and it may help to write your answers down. And of course, I'll be leaving you with an invitation to return – this book wants to work hard for you, so please allow it to do just that!

Where are you now?

By now, I hope you've found enough information and guidance to enrol you in the opportunity of coaching, perhaps as a general style you could develop at work, or simply as something you could use with certain people or situations. Your challenge now is to continue your journey and blend coaching principles naturally into what you do every day. Here's where you might be, in terms of thoughts and feelings.

> Your challenge now is to continue your journey and blend coaching principles naturally into what you do every day

- I know it's something I need to do, and I do understand the general concept, but I'm not sure I can do it naturally in all situations. I'm a bit worried about what people might think if I suddenly start behaving differently.

- I've been trying to remember to do this stuff, and sometimes I do – but to be honest it's too easy to slip into my old style of managing, especially when things get hectic.

- I'm really interested in doing it, but I just can't see where I'm going to apply it.

- Some days I think I've got it, others I don't – I'm having good days and bad ones.

- I've got it! I'm already doing it – it suits a lot of my personality and style anyway – so I'm just going to build on what I was already doing.

As you read this, there is no 'right' place to be: wherever you are is just wherever you are. No matter which of the previous statements resonate most with you, you're in a perfect position to move forward from there. And don't forget that before you picked up this book you functioned with an existing set of skills, and those skills are all still with you. Your opportunity now is to build on those skills and to create more flexibility around people and situations.

 Pause and reflect

Where are you now?

Use the following questions to consider what you want to focus on now. If it helps, write down your answers.

Q Of all the ideas and information in this book, what are the things that really resonated with you the most?

Q What single idea 'bothered' you the most, for example, you didn't like it, were bugged by it, and so on.?

Q **If you could change one thing about your style at work, what would it be?**

Your responses will help you identify the key opportunities for you to learn new behaviours and get better results. For example, maybe the idea of having to develop rapport with people really irritated you as you felt it was all too 'touchy-feely'. Perhaps you're bothered by this because currently, you're uncomfortable with having to relate to (or connect with) people in this way. I'd offer that your frustration is pointing to a potential weakness in your managing style and so is an opportunity to learn.

Where would you like to get to?

Having reflected a little on where you are now, you can now consider how far you'd like to develop your coaching skills. You may relish the opportunity to adopt coaching as a consistent way of behaving at work. Or it might be that becoming a 'completely coaching manager' just isn't for you. But maybe you've recognised that being a better listener might help, or that asking some smart questions in situations would add value. As always, you are the best judge.

 Pause and reflect

Create a sense of possibility

Consider the following questions to help you decide what benefits are available to you now.

Q If you coached people around you more often, what would be different?

Q Of the skills you've read about (building rapport, listening, questioning, flexible styles of influence and giving feedback), which would make the biggest difference if you got better at it? What would improve?

▶

Q What career goals do you already have? Which of the coaching skills can help you achieve those?

Now imagine that whatever you decided you wanted has come true. For example, it's over a year from now and you've been using coaching skills for a while – what's changed? Think both about how things might feel and how other people might be different, for example how they might react to you. Write down any thoughts that occur.

How are you going to get there?

Having thought a little about your destination, let's look more closely at the journey ahead. Think about the things you'll be doing to learn the skills you've decided you want. Now write down a list of those things, keeping it simple and practical. For example:

- I'm going to practise being 'present' to people, to improve my listening.
- I'm going to tell my team to stop expecting me to give them answers all the time.
- I'll be holding more regular one-to-one meetings.
- I'll be asking more questions in conversations.
- I'll be asking for feedback on my management style.

What might stop you?

As we endeavour to create change, life will normally challenge us with barriers or obstacles to overcome. By thinking a little about what might stop you from learning the skills you want, you can be ready to move through anything standing in your way. Perhaps that's your own laziness in a situation, for example wanting to give quick and easy answers rather than working harder to help someone get to their own. If you know that you have the tendency to 'do the easy thing' in a situation, at least you can spot it when it crops up and say 'Aha – I knew I'd want to do this – now, am I going to let it stop me?'

 Pause and reflect

What might stop you?

Reflect on the following to help you identify your potential barriers to progress.

- **Q** So far, what has stopped you from adopting the coaching behaviours, for example as you were reading this book?
- **Q** Of the skills you've read about (building rapport, listening, questioning, flexible styles of influence and giving feedback), which are you going to find most tough to tackle? Why?
- **Q** What's the main thing that might stop you from bringing coaching skills into your everyday style?

When you've got answers to these questions, think a little about what you might do to overcome those barriers, writing your thoughts down if that helps. Sometimes it's enough just to acknowledge the barriers as, somehow, recognising them can diminish them.

Support your ongoing learning

Spend a little time thinking about what support you need for your journey of learning and development. Maybe you like reading or listening to audiobooks, or maybe you're more action based and like attending training courses. Maybe you learn from other people, such as a colleague or mentor or coach. Some people like to keep a learning diary, writing down their thoughts and experiences to help them focus on a topic. We learn in different ways, so be creative and decide how you will support and sustain your learning going forward.

Free materials: learnstarr.com

If you decide to continue your development with this topic, there are free-of-charge downloads and materials to view on my website: **www.learnstarr.com** Simply look in free download areas (watch, listen etc.). There you'll find videos, exercises, routines and descriptions that can help you practise and strengthen your skills further.

Available to purchase: Brilliant Coaching Video collection

On **www.learnstarr.com** you'll also find a collection of videos to teach and demonstrate the ideas and principles from this book (this is a paid-for resource). I explain this book's key ideas and principles and you can also watch Response Coaching, the Steppingstones Model and the core skills and so on brought to life by coaches and actors.

In a nutshell

Take your learning forward

So, you've reflected a little on where you are now, where you'd like to be and also upon the journey ahead. By understanding the benefits of strengthening your skills further, I hope you're motivated to tackle any of your challenges along the way. The simple skills of building rapport, listening, questioning, flexible styles of influence and being able to offer constructive feedback will equip you not only to coach but to operate successfully in whatever role or career you choose.

I'll close by saying that I hope that this book has supported the work that you do – please revisit any time, and I wish you every success with your coaching!

Index